Airbnb on Autopilot

Automate 5-Star Service

Save Time & Boost Profits
for your Vacation Rental

READER BONUS

While there isn't a "u" in "book", there should be! This book wouldn't be possible without YOU. To show my appreciation for your time, I'd like to share a special bonus with *Airbnb on Autopilot* readers.

Goodies Galore!

- Superhost Message Sequence PDF: Easy Copy and Paste Format
- Vacation Rental Essential Supplies Checklist
- Vacation Rental Cleaning Checklist

Visit **www.JTMcKay.com/autopilot** and grab your freebies now! Yes, I'll ask for your name and email, but only to reach out with updates and future books you may be interested in. Since I despise Spam as much as you, I promise to never share or sell your info. It's in safe hands.

Airbnb on Autopilot

J.T. McKay

Copyright © 2021 by J.T. McKay

Published in the United States by Wonder Ridge

All rights reserved. No part of this publication may be reproduced, stored or transmitted in any form or by any means, electronic, mechanical, photocopying, recording, scanning, or otherwise without written permission from the publisher. It is illegal to copy this book, post it to a website, or distribute it by any other means without permission.

The advice and strategies found within this book may not be suitable for every situation. This work is sold with the understanding that neither the author nor the publisher is held responsible for the results accrued from the advice in this book. For informational purposes only.

ISBN: 978-1-7376033-0-6
eBook ISBN: 978-1-7376033-1-3

What the Heck's in this Book?

1 • Who Should Read This Book?	1
2 • Before You Press AUTOPILOT	5
3 • Introduction	13
4 • Importance of Authentic Automation	19
5 • Easy Automation Tools	29
Management Automation Tools	29
Home Automation Tools	41
6 • Your Bestselling Welcome Book	51
7 • Superhost Message Sequence	61
Message One: Booking Inquiry	65
Message Two: Booking Confirmation	69
Message Three: Before Check-In	73
Message Four: Check-In Info	77
Message Five: First Morning Outreach	87
Message Six: Check-Out Reminder	91
Message Seven: Review Reminder	93
8 • How to Automate Airbnb Messages	97
9 • Advanced Autopilot Hacks	105
10 • Next Steps	115
11 • Supercharge Your Business	123
Reader Bonus	125
Resources	126
About the Author	127

Who Should Read This Book?

I get it, you're busy superhosting your way to financial freedom. Since time is our most valuable non-renewable resource, I want to respect yours. Let's find out if plowing through *Airbnb on Autopilot* is a good use of your precious tick tocks.

Are you tired of:

- ✓ Answering every guest message
- ✓ Updating calendars and prices across multiple booking websites
- ✓ Doing key hand-offs for each check-in
- ✓ Remembering to send review reminders after check-out

I hear you! There must be a *smarter* way.

Even though timesaving tools existed when I started, I didn't know about them. We're called "newbies" for a reason, right? I started following BnB breadcrumbs that would not only rock my hosting world, but AUTOMATE it, too.

I wrote this short but helpful book to liberate my fellow real estate entrepreneurs from the shackles of time-sucking minutia inherent in running a short-term vacation rental business. What follows is my exact blueprint for breaking free from "always on" hosting.

While "Airbnb" is in the title, it's a catch-all for anything related to short-term rentals (STR). The information presented is platform-friendly and will work on your fav booking site.

Who SHOULD Read It?

Dive into this info-packed book if you want to learn tips and tricks to automate 85% of your STR empire and show the clock who's boss. Give it a read if Automating with Authenticity is important. Creating a personal connection with every guest has been key for me to improve rankings and steadily grow revenue. It's the backbone of my 'Guest First' Framework.

Since value is subjective, I believe the following investors will walk away with immediate, actionable ideas from this book:

> **The beginning host.** New to the high-flying world of STRs? As you're discovering, it's unlike any other real estate investment. While the potential for 2-3x profits over long-term rentals is very real, it comes with a price: time. Since anything of value takes effort, I want to arm you with the proper playbook to maximize your return on time investment.

> **The part-time host.** Only occasionally flip-on the For Rent sign? Why not up your rental game and implement practical strategies to lighten the load and increase revenue? Just because it's part-time, it shouldn't feel like full-time work.

▷ **The seasoned host who wants to learn more.** If you've been hosting for a couple years, but know there are opportunities to fine-tune the short term machinery, then this book could be a nice fit. While you live and breathe the fundamentals, I hope my framework can build upon your existing experience.

▷ **The long-distance host**...like me! It was sink or swim in a pool at a tropical resort while my biz ran on autopilot. Thousand of miles stood in the way of being a hands-on host. Early on, it wasn't easy. Where was this book?! Automating the invisible money maker was a must. Systems and specialized tools helped bridge the distance. For all my long-distance peeps, I got you and look forward to "showing you the way".

▷ **The host who wants more money.** Do you use a property management company? Are you happy giving away 20-40% of the profits? Many new hosts are intimidated by all the *perceived* moving parts of hosting. Hiring a manager to insulated oneself from potential drama and overwhelm is a common move. Hopefully, this book will give you the confidence to give self-hosting a try and put more money where it belongs...in your pocket! After giving it a go and you still hate it, no worries, a property manager would love to drop their hook back into your revenue stream.

Binge Watch Your Fav Show Instead

See yourself on the list? Sure, it's somewhat broad. I am trying to sell books after all. BUT, it's not for everyone. Since I don't want to waste anyone's time, it may not be a good fit for:

- **The management pro.** If you manage multiple properties with ease using your own automated systems and solutions, you probably don't need this book. Keep up the great work!

- **The hands-off host.** Does another company manage your property? If you're happy with their services, great! In my experience, most management companies aren't worth their high fees. Hopefully, you have a good one! Whatever you do, shop around for the best rates and reviews. Do they include cleaning fees, light maintenance and marketing in their fees? If you're forking over 20-40% of your revenue, make sure top notch service and guest satisfaction is included.

- **The control-loving host.** Do you cringe at the thought of turning over your business to "robots"? Must every guest message, no matter how repetitive, come from you? Is technology a foe and not a friend? If investing time in the daily tasks required to run an STR business is more comfortable than flipping on the autopilot switch, then stay the course. No need to upset the balance. If it works for you, that's what matters.

If you're still with me, great! I'm looking forward to sharing the view from the cockpit as we explore ways to host smarter, not harder. I promise not to hold anything back.

Not only will I share ideas and methodology, but my message templates for guest communication. If you're ready to wrestle back precious time and turn your short-term rental business into an automated, profit-generating machine, buckle up and get ready for take off.

Hopefully, the drink cart shows up soon. This material is better when sipping something frosty.

Before You Press AUTOPILOT

BEFORE pressing the big, red autopilot button, it's imperative your, literal and figurative, house is in order. There's no value in automating outdated or substandard systems. Don't hold your breath for a self-driving Pinto. Resources, like time and money, should only be invested in profit-producing products.

Your vacation rental business can be split into two categories:

- **Product**: The property or space you rent.
- **Marketing/Sales**: Actions focused on selling your product.

Optimal results rely on both being fine-tuned. If either is out of balance, your Cash Flow Machine will break down. You may have a jaw-dropping product, but piss poor marketing/sales engine OR awesome marketing/sales platform, but a product even cockroaches avoid. [Cue the Price is Right loser buzzer. Sorry, no Showcase Showdown, Martha.]

Just like you wouldn't paint a house red-tagged for demolition, don't activate any of the upcoming automation strategies until you've mastered the fundamentals of the short-term rental biz.

If you're fresh on this exciting trail, join me as we dig into what that looks like. It's not as daunting as you think.

Pre-Automation Checklist: Product

☐ **Guest-ready property.** Before turning on the "For Rent" sign, make sure your space is five star worthy. What does that mean? It must be clean, comfortable, stocked with basic amenities, resemble the listing photos and meet expectations.

Guests aren't expecting a $1125 De'Longhi Espresso Machine. They are counting on comfy towels, decent linens, nice bed and hotel-clean space. Your listing should set proper expectations to avoid unpleasant surprises.

☐ **Rockstar local team.** Your product is only as good as the team members who keep it running. This is especially true if you're hosting from a distance, like me. Without five star local cleaners and maintenance crews, our rental business evaporates.

For local hosts, run the numbers and evaluate how much is your time worth. Once your product is producing a nice return, does it make sense for you to scrub floors and launder linens?

Regardless of who's breaking a sweat to ensure your space is clean, operable and safe, it's fundamental to have this piece dialed-in.

Instead of one handy person on speed dial, find four. The good ones are busy. Your business is only as strong as your team. Choose wisely and be ready to pivot if necessary. It's impossible for a human team member to be "Employee of the Month" every month.

SUPERHOST TIP

Reliable cleaners and maintenance crews can be as elusive as a sax playing unicorn. Tough to find, but such sweet Kenny G when you do. Whether you host from 2000 miles or two blocks away, good resources for locating top local talent include:

- **Facebook Groups**: Search your area/city and "Vacation Rentals", "VR", "Short Term Rentals", "Vacation Rental Owners" or "Airbnb". Usually, you'll find a helpful group of like-minded owners happy to make recommendations. Proper etiquette dictates you give as much as you take. Make sure to actively contribute to the group. Groups like these have saved my hosting hide during plumbing emergencies, freak snow storms and anytime I need an answer only a more experienced host would know. One day, you'll be in a position to throw out the virtual life-preserver. Sharing is a must for success in this business.

- **Meet-Up Groups:** Research local vacation rental groups that hold in-person or virtual meetings. This is a great way to make connections and develop a strong local network. Check Meetup.com to see if groups for your area exist. If not, why not start one?

- **Local STR-Focused Realtors**: Early in my investing career, I assumed all realtors were cut from the same pant suit material. During open house tours, they'd try to sell me on the dream of living in the space. "Imagine, what a splash of Driftwood Dandelion paint would do? Can't you imagine reading the newspaper on this toilet with a picture window view of the backyard? Pure heaven."

Uh, no. The only thing I'm focusing on: Will it cash flow?

Most residential realtors aren't investor-savvy. Sure, they can sell you a house, but it doesn't mean it's a fit for short term rentals. Today, I only work with realtors who are investors themselves and understand the nuances of the business. They're a great resource for not only contacts to build your team, but can keep you abreast of local STR news and regulations.

Don't wait until after you close escrow to ask for recommendations. Make sure they're open to sharing their contacts before you decide to work together. Assembling a trustworthy team is as important as buying the right property.

Pre-Automation Checklist: Marketing/Sales

☐ **Solid rental listing on your booking platform(s) of choice.** I resisted using "wow-worthy" or "head turning" listing. For new hosts, it's a tad intimidating. Our goal is to get you up-and-running as quickly as possible without sacrificing quality.

A solid listing must have: Professional-looking photos, eye-catching headline, engaging description and competitive pricing.

Since you judged this book by its cover before taking the "Buy Now" leap, your potential guests will judge your featured image and headline. In a sea of competition, your listing has to POP. Slowing the scroll of an impatient shopper is a mighty task.

Your feature image and snappy headline has to channel its inner Sumo wrestler and transform a scroller into a clicker. Once you have them by the mouse, dazzle with more photos and engage their imagination with your personal and inviting listing description.

SUPERHOST TIP

There's a reason Airbnb and other booking sites allow thousands of characters of text on your listing page. You're not listing a used toaster oven on Craigslist. You're selling a dream. Planning a vacation is incredibly personal. Your images and text must activate a shopper's fantasy reflex. Your story must draw them in and evoke FOMO (fear of missing out). If they don't book now, someone else will get to live their fantasy.

Each of my listings bulge with over 3000 characters (about 550 words). Not only do they paint a fun picture, they disclose positive and negative details of the space. Travelers abhor unpleasant surprises.

The more transparent your listing, the less guest drama in your future. Notice I said "less", not "none". The one constant in this biz is uncertainty. You never know who will call your space "home".

Avoid Starring in a Horror Story

We've all heard Hosting Horror Stories. In my unscientific research, I've discovered one variable which increases the horror story odds: Short, impersonal listings. Operating under the "like attracts like" theory, I prefer people who have the patience to read a good story.

If my wall of text is a turnoff, perfect! I'm sure you'll find a 13 word listing perfect for trashing. (Wow, snarky. Really need another cup of bourbon...uh, coffee.)

You're free to challenge my theory, but is it worth the risk? In good conscious, I can't/won't endorse lackluster listings. Refer to my earlier statement:

> *The viability of your business depends on both your product and marketing/sales machinery being fine-tuned.*

Who cares if your product is the sweetest on the street if it can't attract a booking. Take time to put the right amount of shine on your listing and you'll smoke a majority of your competition. While this book doesn't focus on best practices for listing enhancement, there is no shortage of opinions online.

Flip the Autopilot Switch

Before we take off, one last check of your vital components:

- ✓ **5 Star Property**-Ready to delight guests
- ✓ **5 Star Team**-Ready to keep your property safe, clean and comfortable
- ✓ **5 Star Rental Listing**-Ready to attract and convert the right customers

Looking good! I can't wait to juice this jumbo jet and get air bound. There are so many timesaving and ranking-boosting automation techniques to share.

Buckle up. We're off!

Introduction

ASK any successful entrepreneur how they scaled beyond a one person operation and they'll say: Systems. They implemented systems to handle repetitive, non-revenue generating tasks.

What used to be zombie brain sucks, task-specific systems now tackle on autopilot, freeing them to invest time in profit-producing activities.

There's nothing tastier than entrepreneurial brains for zombies. Nobody works harder than a small business owner. Many feel like they must wear every hat in the closet. No matter how minuscule and mindless the assignment, they're on it!

For zombies, it's like shooting silverfish in a barrel. For too long, they've had a free pass to the All-You-Can-Suck Brains Buffet.

The two most valuable assets? Your brain and time. Today, technology has made it easy to protect both. If it's never been so simple, why are zombies still dining in our home office?

While everyone loves a good zombie analogy, what the heck does this have to do with short-term vacation rentals?

Hmmm, only *everything*.

Whether you're pulling the levers on over 100 properties or renting out your spare room, you are a real estate entrepreneur. If you haven't already, pop the cork and celebrate your awesomeness. I know I will. Sure, any excuse to pop a cork, but I'm proud you are prioritizing 'passive' income generation.

Ha, that's a good one!

Unless you're investing in real estate REITS or syndication deals, there's nothing PASSIVE about the endeavor. Generally, long-term rentals (single tenant on a lease) are more passive than short-term rentals.

If anyone's in desperate need of a super-sized Easy Button, it's the haggard host. Without automated systems, you're chained to the virtual front desk 24/7.

Whatever you do, don't open the calculator app and compute your hourly salary. You'll definitely be popping corks, but not for the right reasons.

Big Time Dummy

How is a new host expected to know better? I didn't. I was a big time hosting dummy when I started. Short term was an exciting new world. I was a seasoned long-term investor when I stumbled into my first vacation rental cabin.

"Stumbled" being the key word. I had zero intention of running a vacation real estate business. On paper, that sounds awful.

I found an investor on Bigger Pockets who was in a market I was researching for investment opportunities. She agreed to a phone call. Halfway through, she inquires, "Have you ever thought of buying a cabin in Pigeon Forge?"

First, I have a non-negotiable investing rule: Never invest in a city with "Pigeon" in its name. Sorry, a zip code full of winged rats isn't appealing. I told you I was a dummy.

"Pigeon, what?," I replied with a healthy dose of attitude.

"Oh, Pigeon Forge. You know, Dollywood, Gatlinburg, The Great Smoky Mountains. It's only the number one vacation destination for families," she said.

Duh, I knew that.

I may be a dummy, but I'm a self-aware dummy. Immediately, I saw the error of my limited thinking and pivoted.

After hanging up, I hit some real estate websites. Wow, it's really a thing…or 'thang' as they say in Pigeonville.

Cuckoo for Cabins

These cabins were beautiful. I was smitten and had to have one.

What happened next broke my biggest rule in real estate investing: Don't buy a property without kicking the tires.

I'm amazed how some buy properties sight-unseen all over the world. I can understand if you have a trusted source on the ground, but many times you're clueless to what you're stepping into. It's not always a pot of Bitcoin, either.

I know plenty of successful investors who aren't as anal about this, but I need to verify it has walls and a roof. Call me nutty, but I enjoy buying properties that won't implode as soon as I wire the down payment.

Within the hour, I found the perfect cabin and the top realtor to take it down. 24 hours later, my offer was accepted and I booked a trip to do some log kicking.

It's rare properties live up to their photogenic hype, but this charmer did. Except for minor repairs, it didn't require any major work. 30 days later, I was in the short-term rental biz.

Anyone who has a performing property won't be shocked to learn, a year later, I bought my second cabin. That's me on a 20' ladder installing a canon to theme it out. Theming your space is chock full of opportunities and is a topic for another book.

Bottom line: These cabins have outperformed my long-term rentals by a multiple of 200-400. Jaw-dropped, I had no idea how powerful the Pigeon was.

Dummy No More!

I don't type this to brag and I'm far from the most successful Airbnb host, but two one bedroom cabins gross over $100,000 annually. Like I said, this is on the low end. There are people with larger cabins pulling down over $250k+ a year.

Authors or scammy marketers who trumpet exaggerated profits are a turnoff. Usually, the numbers are from people in situations unlike mine. Take this with a grain of pink sea salt. Your results will vary depending on too many factors to list.

One significant factor, however, is usually out of our control: timing. When you buy can be just as important as where you buy. I happened to "luck" into the cabin purchases before the market exploded. Today, I probably wouldn't drop $350/sq foot for the same cabin.

If you haven't sealed the deal on a property yet, I feel your frustration. Markets across the country are lava hot. If buying doesn't make sense now, consider other creative acquisition strategies, like rental arbitrage. Haven't heard of it? The short story: Convince a landlord to lease a property to you for use as a short term rental. Lately, there's a lot of hype around this strategy. Make sure to do your due diligence before inking any deals.

While you may not hit the Short-Term Rental Powerball, implementing specially designed systems will dramatically boost your hourly salary. By spending less time on minutia, you can focus your zombie-proof brain power on activities to generate new sources of income.

After a couple months of answering every guest message, I had enough. There must be an Easier Button. Of course there was. Since I was a beginner, it just wasn't on my radar yet.

Today, most of my vacation rental biz runs on autopilot. 'Most', because, like a flight on autopilot, turbulence happens. When it does, the pilot needs to wake up from his nap and take the controls.

BUT, there's even a way to automate your way around some types of "rough air". (Can't stand that one: "Rough air". Just tell it straight...which I promise to do.) All will be revealed.

Enjoy the ride!

J.T. McKay

P.S. When you're finished reading, would you please leave an honest review on Amazon? I'd be incredibly grateful, as reviews are the best way to help others discover this timesaving book. Plus, I appreciate helpful feedback and am always looking to provide more value to readers.

This link will take you to the book's review page on Amazon: **www.JTMcKay.com/review5**

Look forward to seeing your review!

Importance of Authentic Automation

INCOMING! Marketing canons are taking aim at anything with a screen and blasting away 24/7. Splattered with spam, our inboxes and social media feeds are battlegrounds for attention. Only the loudest, most disruptive messages make the cut.

However, from a consumer's perspective...ours! They're the first to get cut, deleted and unsubscribed. While marketers have become more savvy in their messaging, we've become equally savvy in identifying inauthentic, generic messaging.

Cutting through the deafening digital noise isn't easy. As attention spans plummet, we have less time to grab the eye from a potential customer/guest. Have you scrolled listings on a booking platform lately? It's a dizzying display of text and pics. Every headline and carefully selected cover photo competes for the swipe of a credit card.

Brian Chesky, Airbnb's co-founder, is repelled by the amount of "mass-produced and impersonal travel experiences". Creating trust and connection within the travel industry is his top priority. AND, it should be ours, too.

The More You Reveal-The Greater You Appeal

'Authenticity' has become a power word for marketers. Online search has exploded for the term. While most realize they should be doing it, they don't have a deep understanding of the concept. With authenticity, it's all about depth.

Like digging for water, the deeper you go, the greater the flow. In marketing and customer service, the more you reveal, the greater your appeal.

Being authentic is being honest. I hear you, "But I AM honest. I don't lie about my space or amenities." Thank you! Nothing like booking a "charming room for dog lovers" and arriving to find you booked the backroom of a dog kennel with a cot. That's just doggone deceitful. Woof.

Since we each have a unique personality, perspective and voice, the more you infuse your listing, photos and guest communication with that YOU Special Sauce, the more connection you'll create with future customers. People crave genuine connection from fellow humans, not generic spam bots.

If you're trying to appeal to Millennials, younger audiences or people who may not be interested in your offer, honest, YOU-driven messaging has a better chance of hitting the mark. One survey reveals 84% of Millennials don't like advertising at all. They've been marketed to since birth and can spot a fake on any screen.

This isn't just a Millennial thing, research continues to support the idea of consumers' buying decisions being influenced by emotions, not logic. Nothing strikes an emotional note quicker than you being you.

As booking sites become more congested, authentic marketing becomes more critical. It may be challenging to compete on price, location and quality, but you're never in short supply of the U-Factor. No technique is cheaper or more powerful.

'Guest First' Framework

Infusing more 'you' in your short-term rental business may sound intimating. Many investors I know aren't the most warm and fuzzy types. They prefer real estate because it provides some anonymity; at least long term investing does.

If you're self-managing vacation rentals, you better put on your best front desk smile and get ready to become a customer service pro. Instead of being an Activities Director on an oil freighter, you're on the Lido Deck of a Carnival Cruise. Straighten your cap, crack a big smile and focus on helping others have the best experience possible.

When crafting an authentic message:

- **Find your voice.** Are you funny, serious, quirky, poetic, a local expert?

- **Know your ideal customer.** Create a snapshot of your typical/ideal guest. What do they like? How do they speak? What type of media do they consume?

- **Write from your point of view (POV).** This is YOUR listing, give it a unique voice that's an extension of yours. Infuse your personality into every aspect of your messaging.

- **Stay consistent.** Everything from your headline, listing copy, photo descriptions and guest messages should have the same "voice".

While this book isn't intended to provide a deep dive on writing the perfect headline or listing, there are plenty of online resources to help fill-in the blanks. However, I'll go deep when we talk about crafting authentic messages to be used in automated guest communications in Chapter Seven.

The Power of Connection

Imagine the following two scenarios and their potential impact on your vacation rental business.

<u>Scenario One</u>

A family of four is excited for their mountain getaway. It's been years since they've taken a vacation and they have high expectations for this trip. After a five hour drive, with some missed turns and "scary" mountain roads, they arrive. Weary from the long trip, they can't wait to slip into the hot tub and unplug from reality. "Honey, where's the door code?" Everyone scrambles and starts scrolling on devices to find the magic code to unlock their vacation. It's buried in some emails and difficult to locate.

Eventually, they find it and type it in the electronic lock. -BUZZ- Red lights flash. They enter it again. -BUZZ- More red lights. Frustrated, they message the host…you. Hopefully, you reply quickly. After all, they're sitting on the front porch with luggage in hand after driving for half a day. "Oh, I'm sorry. Let me get you a new code." Great, that one worked. They're in!

Uh-oh. The cleaners forgot to start the dishwasher and the hot tub is cold. This isn't the impression you were hoping to make. You do your best to smooth things over, but worry they'll ask for a refund and/or leave a bad review. You have had no contact with them since they booked, so it's tough to get a sense of what they'll do.

Scenario Two

The same scene transpires with not being able to get inside, dirty dishes and icy cold hot tub. While this is disappointing, thank goodness the family of four is your best friend from high school. You have history and a personal connection. Your friendship doesn't make the snafus less annoying, but it does make them less personal. Since your friend trusts your intentions, they're not concerned about the hiccups, as long as you deliver the service and help required. What a relief come review time.

-End Scene-

It's proven, the more connection a customer has with a company, the more likely they are to look the other way when things go wrong. The more forgiving they are is proportionate to the depth of their relationship. I'm not suggesting creating a whirlwind love bond with every random guest. If you do, please write THAT book. I'll be your first customer.

Most feel disconnected from companies they do business with. They feel like faceless numbers on a monthly spreadsheet. As hosts, we have the opportunity to do something many CEOs can't, create an actual connection with our customers.

Like I said, we're not talking about Hallmark Channel Christmas movie connections either. You know, new girl comes to town for a fresh start and within 20 minutes is showered with three marriage proposals, a bouquet of long stems and a puppy.

A Little of YOU Goes a Long Way

Thankfully, your guests aren't expecting much. Most hosts meet these low expectations and rarely establish a personal dialogue. Keep in mind, many of our guests are brand new to vacation rentals. Until now, they've spent every vacation in bland hotel rooms with low expectations of personal service.

Your opportunities to delight are ripe for the texting. It takes so little to make a good impression. But, you have to take time early on to craft the right messages and know when to send them for maximum effect.

When I discovered how to put my rental biz on autopilot, it was a game changer. The income became more passive, freeing time to spend on other business ventures. Plus, my reviews and customer experience rankings continue to grow. To date, I have over 95% five star reviews between both properties.

In the category of Host Communication, I have 100% five star reviews for over two years of hosting. (Airbnb only displays data from a year ago. Date range: 6/3/20-6/3/21)

Guests constantly remark how good the communication is. They feel special and appreciated. As they should. Without them, I wouldn't have a business. I'm grateful for them clicking "Book Now".

While I don't have contrasting evidence for comparison, I wholehearted believe my automated, but personal, communication style is a contributing factor in my success. When things go wrong...and they do!...guests tend to be more forgiving and understanding if they feel like we're in this together. I'm not some random front desk dude working the phones, but a guy with a vested interest in their satisfaction.

Why do they feel I care? They don't know me or I them. Typically, all they know is contained in my messages. But it's enough to strike a personal chord. The messages focus on making them the star, but not in a smarmy timeshare presentation kind of way.

To Know Me is To...

Most will never read my host profile-both on the site and in my house manual. If you're not including a friendly looking pic of yourself along with a mini-bio, you're missing out on an easy opportunity for connection.

My wife also owns cabins and gets alerts when movement is detected by the front door camera. One summer the bear activity was off the charts, so she tuned-in to the live camera feed to make sure everything was okay.

On the livestream, she noticed two girls standing around the front door. My wife was worried a bear was close because the guests were motionless. Eventually, one perks up and says, "Did you see this lady's story? She works on motion graphics for the movies. I think she's famous or something. That's so cool."

Boom. Instant connection. These girls will never meet my wife or even talk to her on the phone, but they now know something personal about her. They're no longer checking-in to a random Airbnb cabin, they're guests of Lisa, the movie lady from Los Angeles. That slight shift in perspective goes a long way in the hospitality industry.

Does sharing that personal factoid insulate my wife from future "guest attacks"? Of course not. If you've been in this space for over two weeks, it's impossible to predict how random guests will act. I've had my share of poopy panted guests who checked-in and out with a bad attitude and share it with anyone who'll listen.

While you can't Dr. Phil your way around unhappiness, you can try to minimize some of its effects with a personal touch.

Automating Delight

"Does automation kill the customer experience on Airbnb?" When I saw this article in my news feed, I had two reactions:

-Sure, it can.

-Hell no!

Shocker. Who saw those coming?

The line separating the two? Intention. If one host is lazy and purely focused on the host experience, lackluster, robotic automation can detract from the experience. Whereas another host can prioritize the customer's journey and create automated systems to deliver value and delight.

Most actions boil down to intent. Are you going to shoot an apple or the person whose head it's on? Your aim determines the outcome. Your intent influences the action.

Whenever you craft a listing or automated message sequence, it always begins with intent. Whose life are you aiming to improve, yours or your guest's? Choosing your guest is win win for you both.

Most guests don't expect more than the bare essentials: address, check-in time, door code, check-out time. Surprise them with info about the area, restaurants, activities, insider recommendations, details about the space and other personal topics and you'll surpass already low expectations. Toss in a couple messages before, during and after their stay and -BAM- you're Superhost of the Year (To them, at least).

Written properly, the guests don't know the messages are running on autopilot. Use some of the personalization features and they'll feel you're typing just to them. There is no sweeter sound than someone's name. Adding it to every message is key to establishing a soft bond. All the automation solutions I will share have this functionality built-in.

"Isn't this faking the one thing you're blathering on about... authenticity?" Once again, intent, my hosting friend. If your intention is to add value and above-and-beyond service with a personal touch, it's in line with creating an honest, relatable guest experience.

Authenticity isn't defined by effort. It takes just as much time to blast out a cold impersonal message. It's defined by the spirit behind the effort. Taking time to prepare messages that will delight are born from this spirit.

Who Gave The Robot a Keyboard?

Automation has a sketchy reputation. Some think of Grandpa Joe losing his job of 30 years working on the automotive assembly line. Those darn robots stole his livelihood.

Accountants lick their green chops at the thought of it. It boils down to perspective.

When I think of 'autopilot', my memory bank fires up the mental projector and plays the classic scene from one of the funniest movies, *Airplane*. If you've seen it, you're probably cracking a smile. Yes, it's when the airline pilots have passed out and a passenger takes the controls.

As he's scanning the hundreds of knobs and buttons in the cockpit, he discovers the 'Autopilot' switch. He gives it a flick and in the empty co-pilot's seat, a plastic doll that looks like a pilot starts to inflate. What happens next? Duh, hilarity. It's *Airplane*, after all.

The kind of automation I'm suggesting isn't powered by steely robots or inept inflatables, it's backed by *you*. You're at the controls at all times. YOU is baked into every aspect of the messaging and marketing content.

The only thing we're removing is the real-time aspect of creating every message from scratch every time it needs to go out. Unless you're looking to improve your thumb-only smartphone typing skills, it's not worth the time suck.

Our goal: Host smarter, not harder.

Coming up, we'll survey the entire automation landscape. It's not just for guest communication. There's an app to handle every piece of the short-term rental puzzle.

5

Easy Automation Tools

TODAY, it's never been "easier" to run a short-term rental empire from your smartphone…while swinging in a hammock with a frosty beverage. If you're not the hammock type, then pick a beach, sink into the warm sand and relax while your properties spit out fairly passive profits.

Some authors make a living publishing paragraphs like those. While I got a little nauseous typing it, within the spammy hyperbole, there is a grain of truth.

Anything worthwhile requires effort. It's called "building a rental business" for a reason. Like a home, building something substantial is hard work. There's no "app for that". Done right, though, it's short-term pain for long-term gain.

Built with a sturdy foundation and quality materials, your rental business will be easier to automate in the long run. I would be doing a disservice not to reinforce the obvious before inviting you to a playdate at The Tech Playground. It's so easy to get distracted by shiny new apps and lose sight of what matters: the fundamentals of intelligent investing.

Vacation Rental Apps Gone Wild

There is an app, website or piece of software for every facet of your short-term rental business. How did anyone dare attempt this before now? Long before the world was WiFi-ed, people successfully rented rooms and vacation properties. Nobody really needs any of this stuff to be successful. If your goal is to make this your full-time occupation, complete with 24/7 guest interaction and constant monitoring of metrics, booking calendars and prices, then good on you for rocking it old school.

If you're tired of being chained to the booking beast and need some old school relief, these automated suggestions are worth a look!

Types of Automation Tools

- ☐ Guest Communication (GC)
- ☐ Channel Management (CM)
- ☐ Price Management (PM)
- ☐ Team Communication (TC)
- ☐ Review Generation (RG)
- ☐ Home Automation (HA)

Low Cost Insanity Relief

When I first dipped my toe in the short term space, there were only a handful of options for automating guest communication. Most were pricey for a single operator, so I wore my thumbs out typing the same message over and over to different guests. Insanity!

There was a better way, but I was too cheap to take it. The thinner my hair gets, the more I realize time is our most precious asset. I had to have a smack down with my stingy stinking' thinking'. The following deal was brokered: If a solution will save me more than an hour a week and costs less than $20/mo, just click 'Buy Now' and move on, dummy. Thankfully, most of these options aren't that expensive. Most pricing models are based on how many properties you have.

Full disclosure, I haven't used all of these. The services mentioned get good reviews, though. Like anything recommended in this book or anywhere you consume bits and bytes, kick the tires before buying.

Let's discuss what each tool does and whether you need it. Just because a hardware store has 18 different hammers doesn't mean you need one of each. Smaller operators may only need one full-featured tool from this entire list.

Guest Communication Tools

Purpose: Automate messages with guests.

Features:

- Tired of writing the same check-in message over and over? Worried you'll forget to send that check-in message? (Been there, forgot that) These tools allow you to write all the messages you routinely send ONCE and set-up a distribution schedule.

- "What's the Wi-Fi code?" "How do you use the thermostat?" "Have any restaurant recommendations?" Use these tools to write responses to the most frequently asked questions. You still need to send

- Some guest communication tools have AI-based features to respond automatically to guest inquiries. When someone asks about the Wi-Fi code, the software detects the keywords "Wi-Fi code" and sends your custom reply. Many allow you to review the response before sending. Nothing kills the authentic vibe faster than a robot providing the wrong answer to a guest's question. Game over. The guest is on to your automated ways. Always make sure your automated solutions are truly that: solutions. A guest shouldn't have to ask twice. Rant over.

- Personalization functionality. Using shortcodes, you can insert personal details (like your guest's name) into your custom messages. This is a huge score for keeping it personal! You'll see this in action when we jump into customizing your message sequence.

Who Needs This?: YOU. Every host on this planet and planets not covered by Airbnb. There isn't any reason not to automate your messaging. Sure, you can't automate every interaction, but you can for 90% of them. What will you do with all that extra time? Look for another rental property? Good answer!

Channel Management

Purpose: Automatically distribute property listings across multiple booking channels/websites (Airbnb, VRBO, etc.) while simultaneously managing rates, availability and booking calendars.

Features:

- Avoid double bookings. These tools will update your booking calendars across all booking websites. When a reservation is confirmed on Airbnb, they will block your calendars on VRBO, Expedia, Booking.com and more.

- Change prices across all channels. Change prices and booking details for every booking platform you use in one place. Some offer rule-based pricing tools to help customize a pricing plan.

- Increase bookings. Some channel managers have access to over 50 booking websites/channels. This increases your listing's visibility and chances for getting booked.

- Single Message Inbox. Whichever booking channel or property you receive a message from, it will end up in one convenient inbox.

- Automated Messaging. Most tools also have automated guest communication tools built-in. Don't choose one without this feature.

- Multi-calendar. For multiple properties, you'll be able to view all upcoming reservations on one calendar.

- Custom booking website and payment processing. Some include a custom website for your property and offer payment processing.

Who Needs This?: Some might say 'everyone', but it depends on how many properties you manage and how many booking sites you're on. If you only have one listing on Airbnb or VRBO, I don't see the need. You're not managing multiple calendars. Even if you have a couple properties listed on only one platform, you probably be fine using the channel's interface. However, as you scale with listings and the moment you expand to more than one listing site, channel management is an absolute must.

Things to look for:

▷ Updated API connections. This is tech-talk for: Is the code up-to-date to speak quickly and clearly with the different booking channels? Outdated code can cause delays in synchronization of booking data and could result in double or missed bookings.

▷ Trusted partner of the top online travel agencies (OTA). Look for badges/logos from the top booking sites. If a service isn't endorsed by a channel you use, keep looking.

▷ Customer service. Check reviews to make sure you'll get help when you need it, because you will need it. Hiccups are common during the on-boarding process.

▷ Pricing plan. Most offer two plans: 1) Subscription based (monthly/annual fee) 2) Commission-based. I recommend using a subscription-based service, within reason, because you'll always know how much you'll be paying.

▷ Fees and contracts. Avoid set-up fees and never sign a long or short-term contract. Flexibility is the key. You should be able to cut ties at your whim and not be penalized for it. Legit providers won't try to handcuff you to substandard service.

Price Management

Purpose: Dynamically set prices and update listings across multiple booking channels.

Features:

- ▶ Real-time pricing. These tools will automatically adjust pricing based on changes in demand caused by seasons, day of the week, local events, competition and other factors.

- ▶ Update prices across all channels. On autopilot, these services will not only dynamically adjust prices, but will update them across all your booking sites.

- ▶ Emotion-free pricing. Many new hosts leave a bundle o' cash on the table because they fail to price their space properly. Some feel, "Oh, I could never charge that for my space! Who would pay for it?" Early on, I was guilty of this. Enabling dynamic pricing let's smart algorithms set the price and make real-time adjustments, as conditions change.

Who Needs This?: Most probably could benefit from a price management tool. Full disclosure, I tried one and wasn't impressed. I update my prices manually and probably continue to leave a couple bucks on the floor. I don't mind checking out my competition and setting prices accordingly. Sometimes these apps struggle to make accurate comparisons with the competition. Not every one bedroom cabin is the same, nor would you price each the same.

My advice is to take a snap shot of your prices for the past couple months before taking one of these services for a spin. If you're not happy, you can always return to the old school cave and carve your prices into the walls manually. Most will see a benefit, though.

For clarity, most Channel Managers will update your prices across all sites/channels. However, they won't automatically set them based on previously mentioned factors.

Things to look for:

- ▷ Free trial. Most offer a 30-day free trial to see if it's a good fit. Pricing is too important to risk using a service that doesn't work for you. Try before you buy.

- ▷ Pricing. Two options: 1) Commission-based 2) Monthly fee. You need to run the numbers to determine which model makes the most sense/cents.

- ▷ Channel integrations. Choose a service that works with your booking channels. Most work with the major booking sites.

- ▷ Channel manager integrations. It's important to choose a provider that talks to your channel management service, if you have one.

- ▷ Customizable. Customization is key when setting prices and other booking details, like minimum stays, min/max rates and other fees.

AVOID: Despite the attractive price of FREE, don't be tempted by Airbnb's Smart Pricing Tool. The only people who benefit from its pricing algorithm are guests and Airbnb share holders. Anecdotal evidence supports the theory that it prioritizes occupancy over price. You may get more bookings, but it will be at the expense of your nightly rate. Airbnb's goal is to put heads on beds. Absent from this goal is the bolstering of your bottom line. Move on, you can do better.

Team Communication

Purpose: Automatically send messages and reminders to your cleaning and maintenance teams.

Features:

- Manage team from one platform. Many channel management services offer team coordination functionality. For example, not only will your cleaning crew be given access to your booking calendar, but will be sent automatic reminders of upcoming check-ins/check-outs.

- Task management. Stay on top of your tasks by creating and assigning recurring and one time tasks to different team members.

- App-based. Many services offer apps to make 24/7 management super simple. Whatever beach you're on around the world, you can make sure that living room light bulb was changed.

Who needs this?: Personally, my "empire" runs on text messaging. Since I use the same cleaning crew for both my properties, they prefer text and it works for us. When maintenance issues come up, I text my handyperson of choice. If you're managing over two properties and/or are in multiple cities, you might want to use an integrated team communication tool.

Honestly, it depends on the property location. Some places aren't as high tech and vendors just prefer older school communication methods…like text or phone calls. Rural locales may even benefit from a good ol' CB. Breaker, breaker got your Swiffer on?

Things to look for: Nothing in particular. Most channel management services offer this. Just make sure it has all the features you need…or may need in the future as you grow.

Review Generation

Purpose: Automatically leave guest reviews and send review reminders to guests.

Features:

- ▸ Review templates. Some services provide customizable review templates. It's important for the reviews to be in your voice. You should write two to three different versions and the software will randomize the process of uploading them to your booking platform.

- ▸ Guest reminders. Since reviews are crucial to thriving in this business, sometimes guests need a friendly nudge to leave one. These services will send a reminder based on a pre-set timeframe. Once again, stay true to your personality when you write this reminder. I'll share some examples in the chapter on Guest Review Reminders.

Who needs this?: YOU. Hosts live and die by reviews. Five stars are like rocket fuel. It's important to have a system in place to make sure you're racking up as many excellent reviews as possible. Since I don't trust my memory to send personal reminders to leave a review, I lean on these services.

Things to look for: Nothing in particular. Some guest communication and channel management services offer this feature.

POPULAR SERVICES

Types of services: Channel Management (CM), Guest Communication (GC), Price Management (PM), Review Generation (RG), Team Communication (TC)

SERVICE	CM	GC	PM	RG	TC
Beyond Pricing			✓		
			1% of booking		
Guesty	✓	✓		✓	✓
			Contact for pricing		
Host Tools	✓	✓		✓	✓
			$5/mo per property		
Hosty	✓	✓		✓	✓
			$7-15/mo per property		
iGMS	✓	✓		✓	✓
			$1 per booked night or $20/mo per prop.		
Lodgify	✓	✓		✓	✓
			Price based on # props/$12-48/mo for one		
OwnerRez	✓	✓		✓	✓
			$35/mo for 1-2 properties		
Price Labs			✓		
			$19.99/mo 1 prop | $15.99/mo 2-5 props		
Smartbnb	✓	✓		✓	✓
			$25/mo for 1-2 properties		
Wheelhouse			✓		
			1% revenue or $19.99/mo per property		
Your Porter	✓	✓		✓	✓
			$5-7/mo per property		

*For informational purposes only. Please do your own due diligence on each provider. Prices accurate at time of publication.

Home Automation Tools

Transform your pad into a place the Jetsons can call 'Home' with these super cool home automation tools.

Smart Locks

Keys are SO 2005. Modern hosts rely on Smart Locks to provide keyless entry to guests. This saves time, money and is a big win for flexibility. No more meeting your guest in person to do the key handoff. This is a 'must have' for remote, long distance hosts.

Sure, you could use an antiquated lock box, but why? The problem with lockboxes, unless you change the code frequently, anyone who has ever had the code could get in whenever they want. This is a security risk. Plus, who wants to keep manually changing the code?

No more lost keys, either! The last thing you want is the frantic 1:12am "We've lost the key and can't get in!" message. Problem solved.

Smart locks come in two flavors:

1) Programmable (Smart)

2) Wi-Fi Enabled (Smarter)

I have a programmable lock that's been pretty rock solid for over two years. While it's not connected to the internet, I use the lock's software to generate custom codes based on check-in/check-out dates and times. It's also great for providing access codes to your cleaning and maintenance teams.

Since the lock isn't reliant on an internet connection, there's no chance of losing connection to it. The only downside? You can't remotely delete active codes or get real-time updates when people come and go. That's never been an issue, though.

The big plus with Wi-Fi enabled locks is their integration capabilities with channel management software. They can be programmed to autogenerate a door code and email it to the guest at a pre-set time. This is a timesaver. Plus, you're able to delete active codes in case there's an issue with a "bad" guest or team member.

SUPERHOST TIPS

1. Earlier I took a heartless jab at lockboxes. Realtors, I apologize. I know your industry runs on them. While I don't rely on them for guest access, I have one at each property. They're an important backup if your Smart Lock becomes 'not so smart'. A locked-out guest isn't good for ratings. Make sure there's a Plan B to get them inside the space they're renting.

2. For doors with Smart Locks, don't install a locking doorknob. If a guest leaves and locks the doorknob, you'll end up with a Dumb Door. The Smart Lock will be useless until the doorknob is unlocked. Where did you put that key? Smart Locks come with a dead-bolt lock, which is usually all you need. For added security, consider adding a chain or slide lock.

Popular Brands:

-Schlage Connect with Z-wave (Wi-Fi)

-August Smartlock (Wi-Fi)

-Yale Assure Lock (Wi-Fi)

-Smart Lock-SMONET (Wi-Fi)

-E-Rental Lock (Programmable) My lock of choice.

Smart Thermostats

A major line item for short-term rental investors is utility costs. The more extreme the climate, the higher your bills. Since our goal is to maximize revenue, a tool like a Smart Thermostat can help.

People may be more conscious of leaving lights and the AC on 24/7 at home, but when they step into a rental property, Mom's warning to "turn it off if you're not using it" is silenced. Guests are notorious for setting the AC to 68C before heading out to enjoy the summer day. Ouch, those power bills hurt...the bottom line.

Smart Thermostats allow us to remotely monitor and control our property's temperature using a handy app. Besides turning the system on or off, you can control the temperature and program limits on how low and high guests can set it.

Some even have sensors to detect movement and shut the system off if the space isn't occupied. Be careful with this, though. Guests don't want to feel like Big Hosting Brother is monitoring them.

My 'favorite' are the brain surgeons who turn on the gas fireplace while blasting the AC. Hope your HVAC vendor is on speed time. When the system freezes up, you're going to get an angry call from Dr. Jack Arse. To combat this, I include this warning in my house manual:

> *Please make sure fireplace is OFF anytime you leave the cabin.* | *DON'T run AC and Fireplace at the same time. This could damage the AC & you'll be charged for the repair. No fun!*

Popular Brands:

-Ecobee

-Nest

-Honeywell 9000

-Emerson Sensi (My wife and I use these in our cabins.)

Smart TVs

Guests expect at least one TV in your space. For higher-end listings, expectations of TVs in every room are common. Missing a minute of your fav reality show on vacation won't be tolerated. It's the modern-day equivalent of crops being destroyed by locusts. Bummer.

While providing cable TV is acceptable, today's guest expects at least one Smart TV or streaming device, like Roku or Fire TV Stick. They can log into their favorite streaming service and take charge of their vacation viewing.

Some hosts are cutting the cord and only offering TV with streaming options. The savings are substantial. Cable TV is one of my budget's largest line items and continues to balloon every year. Aside from the cost savings, it feels good to stop supporting these monopolistic pick-pockets.

If you decide to roll cable-free, make sure to provide guests with ample instructions on how to operate the Smart TV and/or streaming devices. This is crucial for older guests who may not be familiar with this kind of technology. No need to suffer a bad review because you didn't explain how to watch televised golf.

One perk of using a Roku TV is Guest Mode. This allows guests to sign-in to subscription channels using their account info instead of yours. Guest Mode prevents unauthorized purchases, too.

What happens if guests forget to sign-out before leaving? No worries! The next guest can log-out of the system or the previous guest can access their account from an app or laptop and sign-out of all active accounts. I include this in my Check-Out Instructions:

> *Please remember to SIGN OUT of any streaming accounts you may have used on Roku (Netflix, Amazon, Hulu, etc).*

Popular Brands:

-Too many to list. Find a model with good reviews that matches your budget. If you don't have a separate sound system, make sure the model gets solid ratings for sound quality.

Noise Monitors

Stop me if you've heard this one...a host gets a booking from a couple self-described as "quiet and in the need of some down time". Hours after check-in, the neighbors are blowing-up your phone with noise complaints and threats to call the police. Hang on, did someone just throw a couch through the window? Party on!

The one constant with this business is you never know who is going to occupy your space. If you're renting a room in your home, this isn't a concern. For remote hosts, this can be an issue. Larger properties are bigger targets for abuse, in my experience. Regardless, I hate hearing stories like this.

One tool to help put the kibosh on loud, unruly groups is a noise monitor. They monitor noise levels at your property and will send alerts when levels exceed your pre-set limits.

Keep in mind, besides the cost of the device, some have annual service fees.

Popular Brands:

-Noise Aware

-Minut (also monitors temperature and humidity)

-Room Monitor

Lights

"Mr. Cabin, turn on the lamp." And the cabin was washed with warm light from a cool Wi-Fi bulb. Too much?

While you CAN outfit your place with a bunch of Wi-Fi bulbs at $10/per, I'm not sure if it's the best investment. Cool things have a tendency to sprout legs. I'd hate to get a text from my cleaners, "The guest swiped all your bulbs."

However, I can see using one or two in lights around areas near the front door. Voice activated, guests can control them with the simple bark of a command. Two other positives: 1) Set schedules for when lights should come on/off.

Guests checking-in late will appreciate the light. 2) Turn lights off when you know the space is empty.

My cleaners used to leave lights on when they left. While it's a nice thought for the next guest, it mainly benefits the power company. If I know the cabin's going to be vacant for a couple days, I don't want any bulbs burning bucks.

Popular Brands:

-Philips Hue

-Sylvania Smart Bulbs

-Many random brands online are Alexa and Google Home compatible

Security Cameras

As a long distance host, after the Smart Lock, the camera is my number two tool. I don't think I could do this without heavily drinking if I wasn't able to take a real-time peek at my property. Not only does it allow you to make sure your place is secure and rules aren't being broken, there's peace of mind being able to confirm the safe arrival of a guest.

It's also great to monitor when cleaners and other team members come and go. As soon as the cleaners finish, I shoot the guest a "good news, the cabin will be ready a little earlier" message. Who doesn't enjoy being surprised with early check-in?

The camera apps are full-featured, too. My camera is connected to the porch light and even has a built-in speaker. If I get a motion alert, I can check the live feed and see if the guests are having trouble with the lock. If so, I could speak to them in real-time through the speaker. Kind of cool...a little creepy, too.

Some cameras have add-on plans which allow you to store the video for different lengths of time. This is important when filing a claim and need proof of a rule violation. Or if you have a break-in, you'll want a selfie of the creep.

Important: Make sure you disclose the use of a camera in your listing and house rules. This is big! With privacy issues front and center, full-disclosure is a must.

Popular Brands:

-Ring Doorbell Camera

-Amcrest Doorbell Camera

-Eufy Doorbell Camera

-Kuna Smart Security Light/Camera (We use these)

Water-Related Solutions

Have you heard the one about the host who has a remote mountain chalet? It's beautiful, but doesn't get many winter bookings. As a result, it sits empty for sometimes a week or more. One guest-less night, a water supply line under the kitchen sink starts leaking. A slow drip turns into a burst line. Only four more days until the next guest!

Painful.

This isn't meant to scare. As long as your property has regular human contact, you're probably fine. For remote homes, leak sensors may be something to consider installing. A little peace of mind during the harsh winter months is as soothing as a bottle of brandy, bearskin rug and roaring fire. With that image, you'll never think of leak detectors the same!

Water-Related Products:

-Leak Sensors

-Smart Water Heaters

-Smart Shut-Off Valve for Main Water Line

SUPERHOST TIP

Whichever smart tool you integrate, provide guests with detailed instructions. Consider recording short How-To videos for some of the higher tech items. More on that in the next chapter. Nothing worse than checking into a home where you need an IT Specialist on speed dial to help turn on a light. That's supremely frustrating and can negatively impact reviews. Sometimes the best option is the simplest. BUT, at a minimum, get a Smart Lock! You're welcome.

How's your shopping list? Don't deplete your kid's college fund to buy all the tools. May prudence and patience be your guide. Actually, teaching a kid how to be a savvy investor trumps most overpriced college degrees.

Interested in these solutions? For ease, I put together a private page with up-to-date links to all my recommendations. Visit: www.JTMcKay.com/resources

Sure, tools are cool! However, one of your most important features is the most overlooked, despite being as powerful as the Asian Weaver Ant. This impressive ant can lift 100 times its own weight.

Wow! Fascinating ant facts, too? Best Airbnb book ever!

Coming up, we're shining the hot hosting spotlight on your mighty House Manual/Welcome Book. Oh, it's a page turner.

Your Bestselling Welcome Book

AN ounce of house information is worth a pound of protection. Protection from frantic late-night phone calls and unhappy guests is one of the many benefits of a thorough House Manual. "Thorough" is the key word. I've stayed at vacation rentals where the manual consisted of a half page of text on a coffee-stained piece of paper. At least laminate it, Kenneth!

What does a House Manual or Welcome Book have to do with automation? When you're making it, nothing! Doing it right requires effort, but we've been down this road. A little short-term sweat will produce long-term benefits.

Shift your perspective from "How much time will this cost me?" to "How much time will this save me?". No need to phone a friend for the answer. A freakin' lot of time!

This small but mighty PDF will perform circus-like acts of strength. It will shoulder a ton of burden well into the future...as it should. You know your manual is a winner when your phone stops pinging with "How do you turn on the sauna?" messages. You don't. That's not a sauna, it's a broom closet.

This is one of the most important amenities of your property. Since most guests will see your manual before your space, it's a chance to make a solid first impression. Impress with attention to detail and generous recommendations.

Nothing says, "I care about the quality of your stay and want to make sure you have the best experience possible" than a well-thought-out House Manual/Welcome Book.

Ingredients of a Bestselling House Manual

1. Cover Page

Include a nice photo of your property. Consider using your featured image from Airbnb, so the guest makes the connection. Add your property's name or logo. I include my cabin's website URL, too.

2. The Welcome Page

The Welcome Page should contain your property's most important info:

- ☐ Property Address
- ☐ Access Information for Garages, Gates, Secure Buildings
- ☐ Wi-Fi Password
- ☐ Your Contact Info
- ☐ Emergency Info

3. Personal Message

Nothing sets the tone for a vacation rental experience like a smiling photo of its owners. Since many guests have only stayed at corporate-owned hotels, it's valuable to let them know you're a real person who also enjoys using the space. When people realize they're renting from real people not faceless Fortune 500s, they're more likely to treat the space with respect. "More likely" NOT always.

I include a happy picture of my wife and me somewhere around the globe with the caption:

Like you, we love packing a bag and exploring the globe. SO many places to see...So little vacation time!

This helps establish a commonality: love for travel. The more personal connection you can create with people you, most likely, will never meet, the better.

Along with the photo, I write a nice welcome message tailored to the listing. Many hosts skip this page. If I haven't made myself clear, please re-read the chapter on Authenticity for my feelings on the matter.

4. Check-In Guide

On this page, there's info about the Smart Lock and where to look for the code. Detailed parking info and turn-by-turn directions are also included. The check-in time is boldly stated at the top of the page. If your space is GPS-friendly and the directions are straightforward, there's no need to provide detailed directions. I do, because one of my mountain cabin's mocks GPS.

5. House Rules & Info

Even though you've provided house rules on Airbnb or other booking sites, it's imperative to reiterate them in your manual. Guests need a document that's easy to access during their stay. You don't want any confusion regarding your expectations for guest behavior. Whichever rules are most important, clearly state them in this book.

In addition to rules, add helpful operational info for items throughout your space. Anything with an On/Off button that has a 10% chance of being confusing should be noted. It's the helpful thing to do. Consider including handy dandy info for things like:

-**Internet**. Sure, you've already provided the code, but what happens if the router needs resetting? Tell 'em how to do it and where it is.

-**Hot Tub**. In addition to warning them not to use soap products in the tub and other disclaimers, there's info on how to operate the jets and temperature control. If the cleaners dump and refill the tub between guests, let them know it still may be heating up when they check in. That line has saved me from an inbox of, "The hot tub's broken." messages.

-**Fireplace**. If you have a gas fireplace, provide details on how to re-light the pilot light. I can't tell you how many calls from chilly guests I've received. Now, I provide step-by-step written instructions and a link to a video on how to fire-up the fireplace. For liability issues, I encourage them to call me if they're not comfortable performing any of the steps.

-**TV**. Remotes, remotes, remotes! SO many buttons! Which to push? If you have more than one remote or input to your TV, explain how to use it. Your guests will love you! Also, remind guests to sign-out of Netflix or other streaming services they may have used. Batteries, too! Where are the spares located?

-Thermostat. While most know how to work a thermostat, it's best to give a basic rundown of your model. Even though it may have similar functionality as their home thermostat, it could look different. That's a phone call in the making!

-Electronic devices or kitchen appliances. Best practices dictate disclosing instructions for any unusual device or appliance, especially if there's a chance of damaging it. Unsolicited advice: Aside from large appliances and TVs, don't provide anything that's easy to break or expensive to replace.

I used to include Bluetooth speakers, but the USB charging cords kept vanishing and guests would complain it didn't work. Bye-bye speaker. Bye-bye complaints.

Unless you're local and can inventory the space weekly, it's not worth the hassle. OR if your cleaning crew doesn't mind. In my experience, they may not mind, but are too busy to monitor all the knick knacks. Sermon over. Anyone want to buy a 'gently used' Bluetooth speaker??

SUPERHOST TIP

Shoot helpful videos showing how to use certain items in your space. On my cabin website, I have a Guest Section with helpful how-to videos for operating the Smart Lock, thermostat, hot tub and TV remotes. This is another opportunity to get creative and showcase your personality. More important than slick production value is authentic communication. When you hit "Record", just be real and have fun with explaining mundane info.

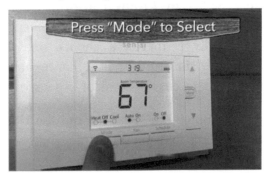

6. Area Essentials & Transportation

Blazing across the top of this page is emergency info and my contact info. Also included:

- Local hospitals
- Grocery Stores
- Pharmacies
- Transportation Info: Taxis, Buses, Ride Sharing

7. Local Recommendations

While the other pages are important to *you*, this page is like a surprise party for your guest. I still get compliments for the restaurant recommendations I provide. You should, too!

Ideas for this page:

- Restaurants. Kick it up a notch and write one sentence reviews for every other one.
- Tourist attractions. If there's a website or place to go for coupons, tell your guest.
- Shopping.
- Local tours.
- Outdoor activities.
- Airbnb Experiences. Do you offer additional experiences like local tours, photography workshops or cooking classes? This is the page to remind guests about them.

While I only offer restaurant recs in my manual, I provide a link to my cabin's website for more area info. I highly recommend creating a simple but helpful website for your property. Not only is it great for promotion, it's a haven for useful info. Plus, you can use it to capture guest info (name and email) in order to build your email list for future marketing efforts.

8. Check-Out Instructions

Front and center is the check-out time. What follows is an exhaustive list of rules and procedures to follow before they hit the gas and take off.

There are more 'moving parts' to renting mountain cabins than city condos. Regardless of your space, think of including:

- ☐ Close and lock all windows and doors.
- ☐ Put away anything used during your stay.
- ☐ Turn off all lights and fireplace.
- ☐ Thermostat instructions for the different seasons.
- ☐ If you require guests to load and start the dishwasher, tell them!
- ☐ Dirty laundry instructions. Do you prefer they leave it as-is or place all used linens in the bathtub?
- ☐ Trash requirements.
- ☐ Report any damaged or missing items to host.

At the bottom of the page, there's this motivational ditty:

Finished With Your Book Yet?

Oh, so that's ALL there is to creating a Welcome Book? "Easy"!

I hear and appreciate the snark. Hey, I've been there... multiple times. 'Overwhelming' is an understatement. Take it slow. While the NY Times may not make space in their list for the first version, keep iterating and improving. A basic version of something trumps a fancy imagined version of nothing.

If DIY-ing a House Manual/Welcome Book causes you to dry heave, outsource it. If you have the budget, pay someone who enjoys graphic design, so you'll be free to focus on parts of the business you enjoy.

Here are a couple providers specializing in digital guest manuals (they all have monthly fees):

- Hostfully
- Touch Stay
- Yoomondo

DIY Option: If you feel graphic design is less painful than a day at the DMV, consider using the online tool, Canva, to create your book. The free plan has enough options to produce something guest-worthy.

Sanity Saver: Hire a graphic designer for a reasonable flat fee to design your manual. Make sure they include the source files, so you can make changes. Find a template or example of a manual you like and ask them to creatively "copy" it. The more direction you can provide, the lower the cost.

Superhost Message Sequence

TRUE confession, this is what inspired me to take fingers to keyboard and write *Airbnb on Autopilot*. The messages you send guests play a big role in your success as a host. Earlier, we examined the power of authenticity and necessity of establishing a personal connection with guests. If that's the goal, this is the way.

As a host, providing quick and satisfying service should be your top priority. There's no better way to achieve this than with timely and personal messages. In fact, the quality of your early interactions sets the tone for the entire "relationship".

Crafting an authentic, guest-centric messaging strategy will pay dividends. Where to begin if you're not keen on relationships with randoms or a fan of creative writing? Over the next eight sections, I'll share samples of effective messages.

Sure, you can copy and paste and be done with it (and I know some will), but don't forget the Power of You. Ideally, you should re-write these in your own style/voice. BUT, you're free to use them as-is.

The Superhost Stack

First, let's zoom out and look at the entire messaging sequence I use. Remember, this runs on autopilot. I'll share the topic of the message and when it's sent. Keep in mind, your settings will depend on your booking rules. For me, I only allow people to book instantly if they're verified users of Airbnb.

Ready to get smacked with the stack?

> **Message One**: Inquiry from Non-Verified Users
> Sent: Immediately
>
> **Message Two**: Booking Confirmation
> Sent: After booking confirmation
>
> **Message Three**: Pre-Check In Info
> Sent: 48 hours before check-in
>
> **Message Four**: Check-In Instructions
> Sent: After confirmation of receipt of Pre Check-In Info
>
> **Message Five**: First Morning Outreach
> Sent: First morning after check-in
>
> **Message Six**: Check-Out Reminder
> Sent: Night before check-out
>
> **Message Seven**: Thanks for Staying/Review Reminder
> Sent: Three hours after check-out

Seven automated messages providing seven chances to forge a personal connection with someone I'll never meet or, most likely, speak with. I hope I don't talk to them!

Not because I'm a cold jerk, but if they're calling, something must have hit the fan. Those calls are rarely cheap.

When they happen, it's another chance to show you care. I've weathered many literal and figurative storms and still walked away with five star reviews. Immediate and caring customer service was a huge factor in "righting the ship".

While your autopilot-ed messages make a good impression, what happens when autopilot is switched off makes a lasting one. Although difficult, always project a Guest First attitude…even when that's all you're getting from them. Attitude!

Sorry, please return to your "happy place". It's time to start slinging the stack!

SUPERHOST MESSAGE SEQUENCE

Message One:
Inquiry from Non-Verified Users

Message:

> Thanks for your interest in our cabin, [guest first name]! I'd love for you to experience it.
>
> One minor detail for bookings with this property, I require a government issued ID to be uploaded to your account and your account to be verified. It's part of the Airbnb verification process & keeps my insurance company happy.
>
> You can find it by clicking your profile picture in the upper right of the page. Then click 'Account' in the drop-down menu. On the left side, you should see Personal Info. It should be under phone number.
>
> Also, the minimum age to book is 20.
>
> Thanks for your understanding. I look forward to hosting you!

This is the message I use when receiving a booking inquiry from someone who's account hasn't been verified. On Airbnb, account verification is determined by whether a user has uploaded their ID. It's up to you to accept bookings from unverified users.

Based on my settings, if someone is verified, they're able to instantly book the cabin. Airbnb has several guest requirements you can select for Instant Bookings.

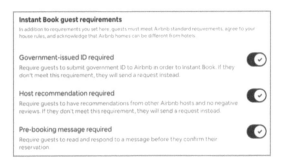

The **Pre-Booking Message** requirement is a great opportunity to learn more about the guest and their vacation plans. Here's my Pre-Booking Message:

> Thanks SO much for choosing our cabin, [cabin name]! A couple questions to help me get ready for your stay...
>
> -What brings you to the area?
>
> -Who are you coming with?
>
> -When do you think you'll arrive?
>
> Thanks!

If you don't require guest verification, consider using a message like this upon receiving a booking inquiry.

> Hi [guest first name]!
>
> Thank you for your interest in our home. This is to confirm I've received your inquiry and will get back to you as soon as possible. In the meantime, if you have questions about the home or area, feel free to ask. I'd love to help!
>
> Best, [host first name]

Keep in mind, for most guests, this message is your first impression. Make sure it checks all the boxes for creating a warm and welcoming experience. You've got one chance to open the virtual door to your home. Make sure the first thing a potential guest sees/feels is your smile.

Message Two: Booking Confirmation

Message:

> Hi [guest first name]!
>
> Thanks for choosing our cabin, [property name]! Can't wait for you to experience it. I'll be in touch 48 hours before check-in with more info. Feel free to reach out if you have questions about the area.
>
> Thanks again! [host first name]

This is my standard booking confirmation message. I have a beach/ship-themed cabin where I have a little more fun with the confirmation message:

> Ahoy [guest first name]!
>
> Thanks for choosing our cabin, [property name]! Can't wait for you to step aboard and experience the fun. I'll be in touch 48 hours before check-in with more totally beachin' info. Feel free to reach out if you have questions about the area.
>
> Thanks again! [host first name]

Some hosts choose to immediate send more detailed info and/or a house manual right after booking. I like to wait until two days before check-in. If someone books three months in advance, do you think they'll remember any of my house rules or procedures they may or may not have glanced at 90 days ago? Unlikely.

In the next section, I'll share my Pre-Check In message and thoughts for using it. Of course, you're free to blast out guest info as you see fit.

Message with Link to Check-In Info:

> Thank you so much for your booking, [guest first name]. I can't wait to host you.
>
> To make sure you get the most out of your stay, I've created a digital guidebook. It contains everything you need, such as check-in info, directions, Wi-Fi code, house rules and some of my favorite local recommendations. You can find it here: [insert link].
>
> If you have any other questions, feel free to reach out. My #1 goal is making sure you have the best experience possible!
>
> Thanks again! [host first name]

In the past, Airbnb has been touchy with sending guests links to competing websites. Specifically, links to your property website. They don't want guests booking directly with you in the future.

To make sure guests receive web-links, consider storing documents in Google Drive or Dropbox. Make sure the Sharing settings in whichever service you use allow for public sharing of your files.

SUPERHOST TIP

Sometimes guests share what they're looking forward to on their upcoming vacation. In my area, outdoor activities are popular. If a future guest mentions 'hiking in the Great Smoky Mountains', I have a Saved Message ready to delight. Keep in mind, they didn't ask for trail info, but proactively providing it scores serious customer service points. I send them links to popular hiking trails with the upbeat sign off, "Happy hiking, J.T.". With a Guest First mentality, you'll discover the opportunities to delight are plentiful.

Message Three: Before Check-In

Message for Standard Home:

Hi [guest first name],

Excited to have you on [check-in date]! Here's a link to the Cabin Manual for [property name]. Please give it a look.

[link to document on Google Drive or other online service]

After you've looked it over, shoot me a message and I'll send Check-In info. (Please let me know if you didn't receive the link...sometimes Airbnb can be touchy about sending links.)

Thanks! [host first name]

Message for Themed Home:

Yo Ho Ho, [guest first name]!

Excited to have you on [check-in date]! We're busy swabbing the decks, getting it ship-shape for you. Here's a link to the Cabin Manual for [property name]. Please give it a look.

[link to document on Google Drive or other online service]

After you've looked it over, shoot me a message and I'll send Check-In info. (Please let me know if you didn't receive the link

...sometimes Airbnb can be touchy about sending links.)

Thanks! [host first name]

These are sent 48 hours before the check-in date. You may wonder if I get a lot of messages asking, "When are you going to send the check-in info? It's a couple days before our trip and we haven't heard from you." It's rare, because in the Booking Confirmation message I set expectations by letting them know they'll receive more info two days before check-in. You're the boss, set guest expectations early.

It's your call when to send this info. If you're more comfortable sending it a week before check-in, great. For me, I want to make sure the rules and check-in instructions are fresh in the guest's memory before stepping foot onto my property.

Not to be an iron-fisted host, but my property, my rules. Everybody wins if rules and procedures are followed. Plus, there's less chance of miss-matched expectations.

Take another look at my messages. Does anything stand out? Am I sending the door code and detailed check-in info? Nope. I ask them to get back to me once they've read the Cabin Manual.

Some hosts put a code word in their manual and ask guests to message the code to receive more info. While I appreciate the sentiment, I feel it can be heavy handed.

To me, it says, "I don't trust you to read the manual, so I'm going to test you." This isn't a good first impression. Plus, even if someone replies with the right code, it doesn't mean they've read the manual. They may have just scanned it for the code.

Superhost Message Sequence

I've had success with this sequence. Granted, it requires disengaging autopilot for a minute to manually send the Check-In Info (next message) once the guest confirms they've received the manual.

If you choose to send check-in info more than a week before the check-in date, consider using a message like this two days before check-in:

> Hi [guest first name],
>
> Your stay at [property name] will be here in no time. How exciting! To confirm, you can check-in after [check-in time] and the address is [property address]. The door code is [custom door code].
>
> As a reminder, everything you want to know about the space, along with helpful local recommendations, can be found in the House Manual, sent last week. Please take another look and feel free to reach out if you have any additional questions.
>
> Looking forward to your stay! [host first name]

The Mighty House Manual

In order to set crystal clear expectations, I disclose the heck out of everything in both my Airbnb listing and check-in info. My Cabin Manual is very detailed with photos, graphics and helpful cabin information. If you don't have a House Manual or Guidebook, I recommend you create one...like NOW.

Mine still gets a lot of compliments. It's another chance to showcase your personality, too. If you're having fun, your guest is more likely to as well. Boiled down, we're in the Happy Memory business.

If you're not comfortable with graphic design or page layout, there are plenty of services who'd love to swipe your credit card. Just search for "digital guest welcome book" or "vacation rental house manual". If you're good with Word or Power-Point, you can purchase customizable templates and DIY it.

Message Four: Check-In Instructions

Message (like I said, it's detailed!):

[guest first name], let's get this vacation started! Can't wait for you to experience our cabin, [property name]. Please review the Cabin Manual, available online, for the full scoop. BUT, for now, let's get you here & inside!

-CHECK-IN: 4PM-

-IMPORTANT CODES-

Front Door: [door code]

Internet Password: [Wi-Fi password]

-DIRECTIONS-

[Detailed directions. Turn-by-turn, if GPS isn't reliable]

[Property Address]

-PARKING-

Park in the driveway in front of the cabin. Because of the angle of the driveway, it's recommended to drive to the turnaround (another :10 seconds) and turn around in order to easily pull-in. Backing-in isn't ideal. It's much easier to back out onto the street and then drive forward.

-BE CAREFUL-

There is a "pot-hole" towards the end of the driveway. It's an access point to the well pump. Please be careful when walking around it and don't trip.

-DOOR LOCK-

Let me in! To OPEN: Enter the ten-digit code and turn the lock latch (under keypad) to the left. Ten digits, are you crazy? You can create an easy-to-remember 3-6 digit Personalized Code. Here's how...

1. Choose a 3-6 digit Personalized Code. Got one?

2. Enter your original 10-digit Access Code.

3. After hearing the tone and while the [SCHLAGE] button is flashing green, press the [SCHLAGE] button and key-in the 3-6 digit Personalized Code of your choice, then press the [SCHLAGE] button to finalize your Personalized Code. You did it!

Note:

a. Each digit must be entered within 10 seconds.

b. If your Personalized Code has been used by another, you will hear the descending tone and see the [SCHLAGE] button flash red. In this case, please try a new Personalized Code.

To UNLOCK using your Personalized Code:

1. Enter your new code.
2. Press the [SCHALGE] button at the top of the lock.
3. Turn the lock latch to unlock the door.

To LOCK from the outside:

1. Close the door.
2. Press the [SCHALGE] button (at the top of the lock).
3. Turn the lock latch to the right until it locks. Easy!

Enter the Wrong Code?

The lock will enter an inactive state for 30 seconds after entering a wrong code 3 times in a row. After :30 sec, the next wrong code will make the lock enter the inactive state for another 30 seconds. Many times a wrong digit is entered. No prob, just wait :30s and slowly enter the code again. If it refuses to work, call me.

-INSIDE-

Yes, you made it in! Now the fun really begins...almost...lets get a couple important things out of the way.

-Please treat our cabin like you would your home. We enjoy using it, too. Report any missing or broken items immediately so I can try to remedy the situation ASAP. I want to make sure you have a great stay!

-Hot Tub: NO soap products in hot tub. No need to pay for costly repairs. | Keep covered

& latched when not in use. | Use at own risk. | *Keep in mind, it takes a while to heat the water after the cleaners re-fill it. Turning up the heat past 103 doesn't speed the process. Please allow a couple hours to heat the water to 100+.

*Due to iron-rich well water, there are brown stains in the hot tub. It's not dirty, just discolored fiberglass. Also, there may be sediment from the water in the tub. It's not dirty, though.

-Unauthorized animals and extra guests will result in the loss of your security deposit, increased cleaning fees & possible non-refundable eviction.

-NO SMOKING inside cabin. Smoke outside with doors closed. Please properly dispose of butts. Smoking inside will result in loss of security deposit and increased cleaning fees.

-Please make sure fireplace is OFF anytime you leave the cabin. | DON'T run AC and Fireplace at the same time. This could damage the AC & you'll be charged for the repair. No fun!

-Use black make-up towels to remove make-up and avoid a $15 white towel replacement fee. Also, please use rags under sink to clean shoes & other messes to avoid this fee.

-Basics Provided: Soap starter pack in each Bathroom (small bar of soap and small bottle of shampoo). If you're staying more than two nights, it's best to bring more. In the Kitchen, we've got your basics covered: salt, pepper, sugar, non-dairy creamer, cooking oil, coffee, coffee filters. Two plastic trash bags. **You'll want to bring more for stays over three days.

-Sleeper Sofa Downstairs: Linens, comforter & pillows available in the wooden cabinet under the downstairs TV. Since it can be a little chillier on the lower level, space heaters are available. If one isn't already out, look in the downstairs utility room (next to laundry room).

-Critter-Free Cabin: No need to tempt critters with tasty treats. Please don't leave food on counters or anywhere within the cabin. Please dispose of trash in the bear-proof trash cage at end of driveway. Don't forget to make sure it's latched closed at all times! Also, don't leave food in car or feed bears. The bears are active and have broken into cars this year (Not at this cabin, thankfully!). Be safe.

-Contact us immediately if something breaks, goes wrong or doesn't seem right. We'd like to fix it ASAP, so you can get back to enjoying your stay!

Since it's a mountain vacation you're after, in addition to all the great aspects, just know it also includes: curvy mountain roads, bugs, bears, critters, snakes, snow & icy conditions in the winter and spotty cell service. It's all manageable, though. You can handle it! Just stay alert and monitor the weather forecast. No refunds for bad weather. Not responsible for run-ins with wildlife.

MOST IMPORTANT...

Have an incredible time at our cabin, [property name]! Please don't hesitate to contact us if there's anything we can do to make the stay more special. Since we're a small family business, we could use all the help we can get with spreading the word. If you wouldn't mind tagging any cabin pics with #[property name], we'd greatly appreciate it!

Wow, that's brutal! I don't think I've ever copy-and-pasted my Check-In Info into a Word doc. I feel for my guests...kind of. Once again: Your house, your rules. While this is an unruly block of text, I've never had a complaint (a couple snarky comments, though) and my phone rarely rings.

SUPERHOST TIP

The more you disclose, the more you manage expectations. There's nothing worse than swinging the door open to your vacation rental to discover it's nothing like the listing. I'd rather be a 'little' long-winded before check-in than on the phone trying to make excuses to angry guests.

Don't forget, this novel hits right after they receive my substantial, yet colorful Cabin Manual. "If they didn't read one, maybe they read the other" is my point of view. BUT, I'm not leaving anything to chance. If there's ever a complaint, it won't be over a lack of disclosure.

Check-In Message Breakdown

Let's highlight a couple important parts of this Info Explosion. Yes, it's a beast, but there's a reason for every line.

- **Most important info first.** The message is front-loaded with the most important info. I'm thorough, but not a sadist. Don't bury door or Wi-Fi codes. Put frequently accessed info at the beginning, like door codes, Wi-Fi passwords and the address.

- **Lock instructions.** If you have a Smart Lock, don't assume every guest is tech savvy. Provide detailed operating instructions. First impressions are crucial to setting the right tone. Two things you must get right: 1) Clear and accurate directions 2) Easy access to the space. Get 'em there and in with as little friction as possible.

- **Disclaimers Galore!** From the pot hole in the driveway to the rust stains in the hot tub to the chilly lower level, I try to pop as many surprise balloons as possible. Guests hate unwelcome surprises, but are forgiving to imperfections. Before I included these, my mailbox was filing up with soft complaints. Peeling off the hot tub cover to discover brown stains isn't the stuff of five star reviews. However, warning guests about the disclosed fiberglass while assuring its cleanliness BEFORE they arrive defuses that surprise bomb. Now, I no longer get those "Is the hot tub clean?" messages.

- **Consequences for unacceptable behavior.** You probably noticed some stern warnings regarding smoking, animals, additional guests and breaking stuff. Guests are harder on vacation rentals than they are on their own home. "Hey, it's a rental!" can be a costly attitude for hosts.

Don't be shy to disclose consequences for breaking key rules. Get specific, too. If a guest ruins a bath towel, let them know the replacement cost. Try to do it in an upbeat way, if possible. "DON'T run AC and Fireplace at the same time. This could damage the AC & you'll be charged for the repair. No fun!" is my attempt to soften the blow of being on the hook for a pricey repair bill.

- **Disclose what is and isn't provided.** If you provide complimentary coffee, condiments, soap and shampoo, shout it from the digital rooftops. If they're travel size or starter packs, mention how many days they'll last and recommend the guest to provide more for longer stays. This isn't a hotel with unlimited mini-shampoos. For many, this will be their first time staying at a vacation rental, so breaking the hotel mentality is important.

- **Contact us if something's not right.** You don't want guests waiting until the night before checking out to lodge a formal list of complaints. This almost guarantees a poor review. Reinforce the importance of immediately contacting you if anything is broken or doesn't seem right.

Some hosts add a requirement to reach out within 24 hours after check-in to report issues with cleanliness or broken items that were discovered upon arrival. You don't want guests trying to blame broken items on past guests when they're responsible. That's the benefit of the 24 hour reporting rule.

• **Free promotion**. It can't hurt to ask guests to use property-specific hashtags when they post pictures of your property. Most won't, but every bit of free promotion helps. You DO have a social presence for your property, yes? Facebook and Instagram are a good start. You can incentivize social sharing with contests or by offering small discounts for people who tag your space.

Message Five: First Morning Outreach

Message:

> Hi [guest first name],
>
> I hope you made it okay and are settling in. Let me know if you have any questions about the cabin or the area. As a reminder, a list of my favorite restaurants is in the Cabin Manual sent a couple days ago. Vacation time is a such a "precious resource" and I want to make sure you get the most out of your time there.
>
> Enjoy your stay! [host first name]

Last section, we talked about avoiding unwelcome surprises. This message is a welcomed surprise. Guests aren't expecting to hear from you after they check-in. They figure you got your money and have moved on to lure the next guest. Reaching out after the first night reassures them you're still engaged and available if needed.

Don't shed a tear if you don't get a reply. Lately, only 40% have been replying. BUT, it is their vacation. Some don't want to be bothered, and that's okay. While you may not get a response, the message leaves a good impression, I believe.

Another perk is being able to gauge guest satisfaction early on. Most guests who reply mention how much they're enjoying the cabin, appreciate the restaurant recommendations and me checking in. If they're not happy, this is an opportunity to make things right.

Engineering even more delight could mean including discount coupons for area attractions and restaurants. Even if you provide a detailed list of restaurant recommendations, you could share the top three picks from past guests. Anything that elicits a response of "Oh, wow, that's really nice. I wasn't expecting that.", is a sign you're on the right track.

SUPERHOST TIP

To supercharge the personal aspect of this message, consider shooting a short welcome video for each guest. Are you crazy? I thought this book was supposed to SAVE time? It is, but never at the expense of creating memorable moments. Imagine your reaction receiving this video message the first morning of your stay:

> Hi, [your name here]! It's J.T., your host. Just wanted to check-in to make sure you made it okay and had a great first night. I'm sure you can't wait to enjoy the day, so I'll keep it brief. I realize how precious vacation time is and want to make sure you have the best experience possible. Feel free to reach out for recommendations for restaurants or things to do. The area is so much fun! I'm happy to share the insider scoop with you. Also, don't hesitate to contact me if something doesn't seem right at the cabin. Your satisfaction is my top priority. Ok, watching videos from Airbnb hosts wasn't in the brochure. I hope you have a wonderful

stay. Thank you again for choosing [property name]. All the best!

I'd be floored if I received a custom video like that. What do you think it would do for deepening the personal connection?

Back to the hippo in the room: time. Yes, shooting these short videos will take extra time. However, it's not time wasted, it's time invested to produce a desirable outcome. Cancellations are rare for me, so my calendar is fairly locked a couple weeks into the future.

It would take a half hour to do a batch recording and knock out personal greetings for the next two weeks for both properties. Same script for every video. The only variable is the guest and property's name.

Delivering this video would require creating a custom Saved Message and adding the right video link. If you're mentioning the guest's name in the video, you'd have to send each one manually. What's that sucking sound? Oh, it's time. The very thing I promised to protect.

It's clear there's value in this idea. How much customer service potency is lost if we remove the guest's name from it? Some, but not enough to not give it a whirl. By making a generic welcome video, you only have to record one and set-up a Scheduled Message for delivery. Super simple and a nice touch.

With any of these tips, I'd love to hear about your experience. Don't be shy. Let me know what does and doesn't work. Shoot me a message: JT@JTMcKay.com

Message Six: Check-Out Reminder

Message:

>Hi [guest first name],
>
>Wow, is it that time already?! I hope you've enjoyed your time in the mountains! Just a reminder, check-out is 11a tomorrow. Please follow the check-out instructions posted on the back of the front door & in the cabin manual. Let me know if you have any questions.
>
>Also, please remember to SIGN OUT of any accounts you may have used on Roku (Netflix, Amazon, Hulu, etc) and make sure the metal trash cage is latched shut before you leave.
>
>I really appreciate you choosing our cabin, [property name]!
>
>Thanks! [host first name]

Who hasn't lost track of time on vacation? Well, not on my watch! Kidding…kind of. This message is a gentle reminder of the inevitable…the transition back to reality. Time to step out of the dream and head back to the real world. Boo!

The timing of this message is important. It goes out at 7p (time at property). Not too early, not too late. You don't want to kill their buzz and send it at noon when they're still living the dream. 7p or 8p is a good time to drop the hammer.

Hopefully, you have detailed check-out instructions in your space and house manual. This is a good opportunity to remind guests of their check-out responsibilities. Many cabin owners require guests to take out the trash, load and start the dishwasher and place dirty linens in the bathtub.

If you have a Smart TV, it's a good idea to remind people to log out of any steaming accounts they may have used during their trip. Occasionally, I get the call for help after check-out with a request to log them out of Netflix. Sorry, I'm 3000 miles away. Just remind them it's possible to log-out of all devices by using the app or signing-in to the provider's website.

Superhost Message Sequence

Message Seven:
Post Check-Out/Review Reminder

Message:

> [guest first name], thanks SO much for staying at [property name]! Please let me know if there was anything missing or can be improved upon. I'm always trying to improve my guests' experience. Your review on Airbnb has a tremendous impact on our family business. As you can imagine, positive reviews are really important...especially for a new cabin. Your review would make a big difference & is greatly appreciated. Hopefully, you had a 5-Star experience!
>
> Please let me know of any areas for improvement —privately— and I will ensure it's taken care of for future guests. Without guests like YOU, I couldn't do this.
>
> Thanks again! [host first name]

For hosts, this is one of the more important messages. Read it again and compare it to what some hosts send:

> Thanks for staying with us! If you're ever in the area in the future, we'd love to host you again. Please tell your friends about our listing.

Ok, that's intentionally piss poor. This is better, but still is missing a key component:

> Thank you for staying with us. It was a pleasure hosting you. We'd love to have you back in the

future. Hopefully, you enjoyed your time here. If so, we'd greatly appreciate you taking a minute to leave a review. Positive reviews help attract more great guests, like yourself.

Thank you!

What's missing? Sign up for my advanced course and I'll be happy to tell you. Don't you just love that one? NO? Okay...

SUPERHOST TIP

The following two sentences are the secret sauce to getting positive reviews...assuming your listing met and exceeded expectations, of course. There's no magic wand to "presto-change-o" unpleasant experiences.

> Hopefully, you had a 5-Star experience!
>
> Please let me know of any areas for improvement —**privately**— and I will ensure it's taken care of for future guests.

You can't directly ask for five star reviews. It's not ethical and violates Airbnb's terms. However, you can plant the "five star seed" with a comment like that.

The real powerhouse is the second sentence. The word "privately" *hopefully* directs any unhappiness to your private inbox and not the public review. We don't want the guest using the public review as a clothes line for dirty laundry. Informing them their feedback will be taken seriously is your final act of caring customer service.

For most hosts, this is the last piece of communication they'll have with a guest. Make it count. After a guest leaves a review, there aren't any do-overs. The cake is baked. Hopefully, it's tasty and attracts others. Avoid bitter batter with a final gesture of authentic appreciation and a soft ask for positive reviews.

If you offer a discount for return customers, this a great place to mention it. Who doesn't feel good after receiving a coupon! That's the perfect frame of mind you want them in before writing your review.

> **Grab the Entire Superhost Message Sequence!**
>
> Who wants to type all those messages? I vowed to *save* you time, after all. Download a handy PDF and copy & paste all the messages. Get them here:
>
> ▶ www.JTMcKay.com/autopilot

How To Automate Airbnb Messages

WHEN I launched my first property on Airbnb, the platform only offered Saved Messages (custom messages you can send from your Inbox). While this saved a ton o' time responding to the same questions over and over, it only solved one part of the autopilot equation.

Automating 85% of your communication requires automatic deployment of messages based on events and schedules. Thankfully, Airbnb heard hosts' weary cries and implemented Scheduled Messages into the Inbox. Huge win for hosting smarter, not harder!

Caveat: Many hosts use other communication tools to automate their messaging and, probably, couldn't care less about this built-in feature. Early on, I was using another service just for this option.

Since streamlining is a goal, the fewer apps/tools, the better. If you only use Airbnb to list and manage your property, the Saved and Scheduled Message features may be all you need to lighten the communications load.

For clarity, let's breakdown the two features:

- **Saved Messages/Quick Replies**: Custom messages you compose and save inside your Airbnb Inbox. Create as many as you'd like to save time on typing answers to the same questions. Some of my saved messages include: Driving directions, Wi-Fi password, breweries and wine tasting info, hiking trails recommendations, etc. Use shortcodes to personalize the message.

- **Scheduled Messages**: Custom messages you compose to be sent on a specific schedule. Basically, they're the same as Saved Messages but come with scheduling options. Every message in the Superhost Sequence could be run through this feature.

What follows are instructions for creating both types of messages within Airbnb. If you use another service for auto-messaging, the specific instructions will differ, but the same principle applies. Consult your service provider's Support section for more details and tutorials. If your Magic Message Machine is already up and running, feel free to skip this section.

Create a Saved Message/Quick Reply

1. Go to your Inbox on Airbnb's website or app. You can access the Quick Replies in two places.

In the message composition section at the bottom of the screen, click the thought bubble icon and choose 'Manage' in the upper right of the next window.

In the upper left, next to All Messages, there's a button with three horizontal lines. Click it and select 'Quick Replies'.

2. On the Quick Replies page, click 'New Reply' in the upper right.

3. Give the reply a name. Guests won't see this, it's to help you remember the message's topic. Compose your message in the message box. Use shortcodes to personalize your guest communication.

Shortcodes allow you to insert variables, like a guest's first name or property name, to help messages feel more personal.

4. Read the message out loud and make sure it sounds warm and conversational. If *you* received that message, would you think it came from a cold robot or kind, caring host? Stumped on the right answer? Go back to page one of this book and try again.

5. Once you're happy, click "Create" and start another or call it a day. You've just spent a little time to save a bunch of it.

How To Automate Airbnb Messages

Send a Saved Message/Quick Reply

1. Go to your Inbox on Airbnb's website or app. In the message composition section at the bottom of the screen, click the thought bubble icon and choose the appropriate Quick Reply. Boom!

Create a Scheduled Message

1. Go to your Inbox on Airbnb's website or app. You can access the Quick Replies in two places.

In the message composition section at the bottom of the screen, click the bubble clock icon and choose 'Manage' in the upper right of the next window.

In the upper left, next to All Messages, there's a button with three horizontal lines. Click it and select 'Scheduled Messages'.

2. On the Scheduled Messages page, click 'New Message' in the upper right.

3. Give the message a name. Guests won't see it, it's to help you remember the message's subject. Compose your message in the message box. Use shortcodes to personalize your communications. Shortcodes allow you to insert variables, like a guest's first name or property name, to help messages feel more personal.

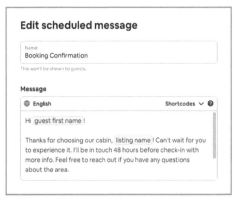

4. Select the Listings this message will apply to.

5. Schedule when the message will be sent based on a specific action and how long before or after the action takes place. For example, to send a Booking Confirmation message, choose 'Booking Confirmed' and then a timeframe when to send. 'Immediately' is what I use. No need to delay a heartfelt "thank you for booking".

What about sending Check-In Info? Select 'Check-in' for the Action and then pick a timeframe that works best. For me, I use 'Two Days Before' and a time of '11AM'. All times are based on the listing's time zone.

6. Read the message out loud and make sure it sounds warm and conversational. If *you* received that message, would you think it came from a cold robot or kind, caring host? Remember to use those shortcodes to add the most important word in the English language, your guest's first name.

7. Satisfied? Click "Create" and write another or pop the cork on something fizzy. You just created your first Scheduled Message. Oh, yeah!

Don't Turn Your Back on the Robots

While it feels great to be free of messaging busywork, early on, it's imperative to make sure your new systems are running on schedule. Imagine the clusterfluck of thinking your message sequence is smoothy running, only to get this frantic guest message, "Hey, we're 15 minutes away from the house and don't know where we're going. Since we never received directions or anything from you, we just started driving to the general area. Please contact us ASAP with more info!!" Wow, massive host fail.

While it might "feel" better to blame it on the bots, who's their owner/programmer? It's on us to verify guests receive the necessary info at the right time. When you create a new scheduled message, double check it's going out at the proper time.

The instant automated messaging becomes a liability, shut it down and find a new solution. Often, this autopilot communication is responsible for creating a first impression. Make sure it's no less than stellar.

Advanced Autopilot Hacks

DON'T let "Advanced" scare you into chapter skipping your way back to safety. "Advanced" is subjective. Some may find these Romper Room easy, others may seek solace in a corner with their fav blankie.

No judgement.

The word isn't solely meant to describe technical ability/difficulty. Some of these tips are next level guest service hacks. Let's get the "toughest" out of the way first. While it requires some tech savvy, the automation benefits could be well-worth the investment.

Automating the Bad Times

Category: Team Communications

Earlier, I teased an idea to automate the hiccups of vacation rentals. You know, clogged toilets, burnt bulbs, cold hot tubs and anything broken. I'm going to share an experimental way to put minor maintenance requests on autopilot while staying in the loop. The goal is to automate, not turn a blind eye on our investment and hope for the best.

Even though the plane soars through the air at 570 miles per hour on autopilot, the pilot is still inches from the controls. You must be ready to take over at a moment's notice. You'll be remembered for these moments.

The Big Picture

Let's start with a bird's-eye view before zooming into operational specifics. Normally when something goes wrong, you get a message or call from a guest. On the fly, you're expected to come up with a fix that's both satisfying to the guest and your wallet. After the plan is hatched, you contact team members to see who's available to make magic happen at 11p.

Wow, that stresses me out just typing it. Why? Because I've been on the other end of those calls too many times to type.

Here's what an Automated Maintenance Request looks like:

1. In your house manual and check-in info, there's a custom website URL to use for minor maintenance requests. On the site, list what you consider "minor". Anything major requires an immediate phone call.

2. The guest visits the site and interacts with an automated chat bot/form. The "conversation" goes like this:

> Bot: Hi! I'm so sorry you're having troubles.
> Let's see if we can't get things sorted ASAP.
> What's your name?
>
> Guest: Joe
>
> Bot: Joe, in case we need to contact you, what's your best phone number?
>
> Guest: [enters number]

Bot: Thanks, Joe! Appreciate that. Please tell me what kind of issue you're experiencing?

-Plumbing -Electrical -Something Broke or Isn't Working

Guest: Plumbing

Bot: Ok, you're having a plumbing issue. Please describe what's happening?

Guest: The upstairs toilet is clogged.

Bot: Again, I'm so sorry you're having trouble with this. I'm going to contact the best team member to address this for you. Is there anything else we should know?

Guest: No.

Bot: Ok, Joe. Please give me 5-10 minutes and I'll have a maintenance specialist contact you at the number you gave me. How does that sound?

Guest: Sounds good. Thanks.

Bot: Thank you, Joe. I'm on it and we'll be in touch soon.

3. When the guest types "Plumber", a text message is immediately sent to a couple team members you've designated as being capable to handle plumbing issues. This message includes the guest's name, number and description of the problem. You also receive the message.

4. Your team starts a private group chat to determine who can get there fastest. A team member is selected for the job.

Since you're part of the chat, you can request specific vendors, if need be.

5. This team member calls the guest to provide arrival information.

6. After the job is complete, the team member sends you a message with more details.

Your participation depends on the problem and your relationship with your team. For certain jobs under a specific price, you can choose to opt out of the communication chain and let the team make executive decisions.

Before implementation, have a training call with your team to walk them through the new workflow. Imagine how much time and hassle this could save.

The Technical Nitty Gritty

At first glance, that may look too Star Treky to pull off for a solo host. Believe it or don't, this automated fantasy can be duct taped together with free solutions available online. What are you drinking, J.T.? I wouldn't type it without first trying it.

Tools Needed

Preferred Solution

Website with Wordpress - If you have one for your listing, you're ready for the bot invasion. Wordpress is a free platform to build websites and has a ton of add-ons.

Form Plug-In - Sure, you could use a fancy chatbot tool, but why complicated things? Use a good form plug-in for Wordpress that comes with conditional logic functionality to mimic a chatbot.

SMS (text message) Integration. Using a service like Zapier, Twilio or Slack will allow you to text the guest's info to your team members. You don't need this if email notifications will suffice. Personally, text messaging is more immediate and has less chance of being missed.

Alternate Solution

Google Forms. Create a Google form to collect guest data. If you don't have a website, you can use a link from Google to display your form.

SMS (text message) Integration. Use a service like Zapier, Twilio or Slack to text the guest's info from the Google form to your team members.

Why is the first option preferred? I'm a stickler for branding and making a professional impression. Nothing says "pro host" like a custom domain complete with logo and simple, but professional website. No, you don't need to sign-up for night classes in Web Design at the community college.

There is a massive supply of pre-made website templates online AND a legion of hungry programmers ready to loving accept your PayPal transaction. If you're familiar with launching Wordpress sites, you could pull this off. Outsourcing all of it could run $300-500.

If you choose to outsource, copy and paste this section and share it with your coder. Sure, there are some moving parts, but it's not a difficult build. Don't let them try to convince you otherwise.

QR Codes to the Rescue

Category: Guest Communications

Yeah, those things! They're everywhere, and for good reason. It's an easy way to connect someone with more information about whatever the QR code is attached to. If you haven't used one, open your smartphone's camera app and point the camera at the code. *Whamo!* A web link pops up and you're taken to a webpage with more info.

I use them around the cabin to provide guests with quick links to more details on various topics. On the refrigerator, I have a Welcome Flyer with the Wi-Fi password and a QR code which connects to the Cabin Manual. There's one on a laminated sheet with restaurant recommendations to take guests to a webpage for more local recommendations of things to do and places to explore.

Another way to provide value is to attach them to objects that may be difficult or confusing to use. They don't have to be big and unsightly, either. You can print a small version on sticker paper and affix it to anything that could benefit from a helpful how-to video or instructional guide.

If you don't like the idea of 18 tiny stickers all over the place, put one on a Welcome Flyer with the message, "For helpful info on our gadgets, just point your phone's camera at this magic code." Stick it on the fridge and proudly strut around in a tin foil hat. You're SO high tech!

The faster you connect guests to the answers they need, the less chance your phone will ring with the opportunity to explain how to turn off the ceiling fan in person.

Selfie-Powered Free Press
Category: Marketing/Promotion

So far, I've spared you the dissertation on the value of social media. No finger wagging. You get it. Many listings can benefit from a robust social media presence. You don't need to post hourly updates, but weekly is a good start. With scheduling software, you're able to plan all your posts for the next month or three.

If you haven't set up a business page on Facebook and Instagram in your property's name, do it. I'll wait. Ideally, both these pages should have the same name. Before I choose a name for a property, I always check the availability of domain names and social media handles.

At a minimum, those are two solid platforms to focus your social energy. If you don't know, you can cross-post content at the same time. Meaning, you can upload a cool picture of your place to both sites at once. Use hashtags in Instagram to increase discoverability of your content.

Ok, enough preamble. To the selfie hack!

While I don't enjoy spending all day on social media sites, I don't deny their importance. Instead of me creating bushels of fresh content, incentivize guests to take it on!

After I purchased my first cabin, a nutty idea struck. Why not buy a basket and fill it with fun selfie props? Come on, who doesn't love wacky selfie props? On some of the larger ones, like an empty picture frame for couples to hold up in front of their smiling faces, I branded it with my cabin's logo.

Did I think any of these cheap party favors would survive more than a month? Heck no. Over two years later, 90% of them are still in the basket! Either people shun them because of their cheesiness OR they're enjoying them. I'm going with Door #2. Guests have commented on how fun they are and some pics have been tagged with the cabin's hashtag.

I encourage you to kick it up a notch and incentivize guests to get creative and post their best selfie tagged with your hashtag to Instagram and/or Facebook. Do a monthly giveaway with cool swag or 10% discounts on future stays. It's a small price for free promotion.

You never know how large some of your guest's networks will be or who they may know. It only takes one influencer to share the post to drive a flurry of activity to your listing. Have fun with this and run monthly themed competitions.

Video Reviews are Gold

Category: Marketing/Promotion

Encourage people to shoot short video reviews and send them to you for inclusion on your sites. This is key. While you can't prevent them from posting bad reviews, if you're explicit with your "contest rules", you can ask for the entries to be privately submitted by email.

Since a good video review is marketing gold, I'd offer an enticement for everyone who submits. Shifting the burden of content creation to guests is a major time-saver.

Make it easy for guests to hit "Record" and give them a template for what to say. I'd laminate a sheet with the following "script":

> Hi, we're [your names] and we're from [hometown]. A couple things we love about [property's name] are...[share 2-3 of your favorite features]. [If you'd recommend it to others, that would be awesome!] We would recommend this place because [share a reason you feel others would like it]. [Any final words? Don't by shy. We appreciate your kind comments!]

Social proof is one of the most powerful marketing tools. Imagine if you start amassing your own collection of social proof videos. Nobody sells your space like a happy guest. Another reason to create a five star space...give them something to gush about.

Next Steps

FINISH your drink. Return your seat to the full upright position. And, get ready to automate your short-term rental (STR) business!

As we prepare for landing, think about everything you just learned and start prioritizing your short and long-term goals. Perhaps you already have a couple pieces of the Airbnb Autopilot Puzzle in place and only need to implement a couple more for a seamless automated experience. Maybe you just hit "Publish" on your rental's listing and feel overwhelmed with next steps.

Whatever stage of the STR game you're in, there are always areas for improvement. When you buy a new car, it's not expected to run forever just because it has fresh oil and a pleasant scent the day you drive it off the lot.

Like your vehicle, your vacation rental requires periodic tune-ups to ensure profitability. After all, it's called a "Cash Flow Machine" for a reason. Oil the gears and check the fluids and the machine will keep you happy.

Whether you're looking to perform a minor tune-up or a major overhaul, first evaluate the effectiveness of your current systems and tools. Ask yourself these questions and be honest with your answers:

- ☐ Are your tools/services performing at the same level they were a year ago? How about three years?
- ☐ Do better, more full-featured tools/services now exist that would serve as suitable replacements?
- ☐ Are you paying for services you haven't used or needed over the past year?
- ☐ Do you have multiple tools that perform the same function? Can you consolidate?

When reviewing current systems and tools, they either provide value and save time or they don't. End of scientific analysis. If you find you're spending a lot of time babysitting and monitoring tools, find new reliable ones.

If the cost of certain services no longer justify the returns, find cheaper ones. Don't overthink this. Tools either add or subtract from your bottom line.

Automation Check-Up

To make this easier, let's breakdown each part of the automation process and examine your current tools and workflow. Feel free to write this down and take notes based on your situation.

Reservations (including inquiries and booked guests)

Current automation tools? Rate each 1-5 based on performance.

Automated messages? How many and for what stage(s) of the Reservation process?

Room for improvement?

Tools to consider?

Active Guests

Current automation tools? Rate each 1-5 based on performance.

Current home automation tools? Rate each 1-5 based on performance.

Automated messages? How many and for what stage(s) of the guest's stay?

Room for improvement?

Tools to consider?

After Check-Out

Current automation tools? Rate each 1-5 based on performance.

Automated messages? How many and for what purpose after check-out?

Room for improvement?

Tools to consider?

Team Communication (including cleaners and maintenance team)

Current automation tools? Rate each 1-5 based on performance.

Automated messages? How many and for what purpose?

Room for improvement?

Tools to consider?

From Diagnosis to Cure

After taking the pulse on your current tools and systems, how do the vital signs look? Spot any time sucking, profit leaking gaps? The sooner you take action, the sooner your Cash Flow Machine can be restored to peak operating order.

My automated messaging game needed serious work. Ha, that assumes I had a game! As soon as I pressed the autopilot button on my Superhost Message Sequence, the effects were immediate. No longer was I tied to my Airbnb message inbox.

Worries of remembering to send guests the house manual 48 hours before check-in or review reminders after check-out, vanished. Savings in both time and stress were immense. And, that's just after implementing ONE tool.

Think about areas of the business you're spending a lot of time in and look for tools to provide liberation. As you've learned, there are options for every facet of this business. Most come with free trials, so there's little upfront friction to kicking the tires on potential solutions. If one doesn't check enough boxes, move on to the next.

When your bottom line is on the line, don't settle for mediocre.

Even if you spend a month setting-up your new automated systems, the dividends they produce will last for years. Don't skimp or cut corners. The stronger the foundation, the greater future growth it will support.

Autopilot Must Haves

For Automation Domination, at a minimum, you need:

- ✓ Solid rental listing. Snappy headline. Great photos. Welcoming description.

- ✓ House manual/welcome book. 'Decent and done' beats 'great and imagined'. This can be improved over time, but it's a must have now.

- ✓ Channel management. If you list your rental(s) on multiple booking websites, this isn't an option. Managing prices and reservations across all sites needs to be real time and accurate. If you only list your property on one site, there's no need for this now.

- ✓ Automated messaging. Aside from a time saver, you'll never worry about a missed message, a missed opportunity for authentic connection with a guest.

- ✓ Smart lock. If you're a long distance host or don't want to be housebound 24/7 while welcoming guests, you need to automate the check-in process. Toss the keys, Kyle, it's not 2005.

That's it! These are the minimal requirements to jumpstart your automated vacation rental business. Let growth and need be your guide for adding new tools.

Like those 128 apps on your phone, you probably don't need all of them. Fine, I'm talking about MY phone. A quarterly app/tool audit keeps you lean and nimble.

Don't Forget to Get Personal

There's a reason I devoted an entire chapter to the importance of Authentic Hosting. And you thought it was to pad the book. No, my hosting honchos, its significance is worth restating.

Tools alone don't make the Superhost. In lazy hands, one could copy and paste robotic replies found online. Superhosts craft super messages. These don't need to be literary works of art, they just need to be personal and reflect your personality. After all, guests have chosen to rent a room from a person, not a faceless corporation.

When I say "personal", I don't mean cringe-worthy over shares. Write your messages in the tone you'd speak them in if you were sharing the info with a good friend. Keep them real and light-hearted.

Being personal or authentic is being sincere.

Since you have a unique perspective, personality and way of communicating, the more YOU reflected in your listing, photos and guest communication, the more connection you'll create with future customers. People crave genuine connection from fellow humans not AI-powered bots. A little YOU goes a long way with making a great first impression.

Plus, research shows people are more forgiving when things don't go as planned if there's a personal connection with the other party. This is the short-term rental biz, after all, expect plan derailments.

Make it a point for your communication to be warm, welcoming and conversational. It may be the one thing that turns a three star experience into a five star review.

As AI-powered solutions become more plentiful and realistic, they'll never be a substitute for a message drenched in your DNA. This is your Superhosting Superpower. Don't take it for granted. Your guests are waiting to be surprised by one of your personal messages. They just don't know it yet.

Thanks for Flying Autopilot Air

Hopefully, you're excited to take the next step and try out some of these autopilot strategies. At the risk of sounding like a broken mp3, they radically changed my STR business.

You think I'd have time to write a book while swinging in a seaside hammock if I was still chained to the virtual front desk 24/7?

While the seaside hammock is fiction, it doesn't have to be. Automation allows you to run your rental operation from any beach, mountain top or couch around the world.

As we come in for a smooth landing, thank you for flying with *Airbnb on Autopilot*. Since you have a choice with business books, it means a lot you took a chance on this one. I wish you nothing but success and clear skies for your business.

Soon, the most pressing question will be, "Where should I put my hammock?"

To hosting smarter, not harder!

Supercharge your Business

BY now, I hope you recognize the significance in implementing tools to automate your vacation rental business. As we established, your first step is to nail the fundamentals and lay a sound foundation to support future growth. There's no point in automating crappy systems, right?

Many new hosts are overwhelmed by all of this. I know I was! Second guessing and 'paralysis by analysis' were two things I could count on. I wasted a lot of time chasing the right rabbits down the wrong holes.

My goal with *Airbnb on Autopilot* was to demystify the hosting process and break it into bite-sized, actionable pieces. Hopefully, it hit the mark and you have a better understanding of the ingredients necessary to creating a tasty five star listing.

If you still feel disoriented, that's normal. Sometimes the best way to get unstuck is to just take a step in any direction. Early on, momentum can trump direction. You can always course correct once you get a little wind under your wings.

If you'd prefer to work with someone who's walked the same path, great! New hosts hire me in order to host with confidence and shortcut the business building process because most are overwhelmed and not sure where to focus their limited time.

So, I help them create irresistible listings to attract the right guests and design automated systems to bolster their business while not being chained to it. Bottom line, I arm them with tools and skills to host smarter, not harder.

Does this sound interesting? Please send me an email if you'd like more info. Since this is hands on and personal, I have only have time to take on a couple new clients every quarter. Regardless, I'd love to hear from you!

Whichever path you take, I hope it's successful and rewarding.

Thanks again for spending time together!

J.T. McKay

JT@JTMcKay.com

Bonus

While there isn't a "u" in "book", there should be! This book wouldn't be possible without YOU. To show my appreciation for your time, I'd like to share a special bonus with *Airbnb on Autopilot* readers. Earlier, I made the case for having an automated message sequence that's personal and authentic. Instead of re-typing each message in this book, I'd like you to have a handy dandy PDF with the entire message sequence and a couple other goodies.

Goodies Galore!

- Superhost Message Sequence-Easy Copy & Paste Format
- Vacation Rental Essential Supplies Checklist
- Vacation Rental Cleaning Checklist

Head over to **www.JTMcKay.com/autopilot** and grab your freebies now! Yes, I'll ask for your name and email, but only to reach out with updates and future books you may be interested in. Since I despise Spam as much as you, I promise to never share or sell your info. It's in safe hands.

Resources

Throughout the book, I've shared suggested resources for automation tools. To make sure the information is up-to-date, I've created a private webpage with the most current links to my recommended resources.

To access the page, please visit:

www.JTMcKay.com/resources

About the Author

J.T. McKay has been investing in real estate for over 25 years. He was a chronic long-term investor, owning properties all over the US, until he stumbled upon short term investing. Now, he's building his vacation rental 'empire' one happy guest at a time.

When he's not dreaming/scheming about ways to automate the real estate business, he's running an award-winning production company in Los Angeles, CA. J.T. loves traveling the world in search of unforgettable sights, eats and stories, too.

Feel free to reach out if you'd like to chat about any of the above! JT@JTMcKay.com

Pretty Please

May I ask a small favor?

If you enjoyed *Airbnb on Autopilot*, would you mind taking a minute to leave an honest review on Amazon? I'd be incredibly grateful, as reviews are the best way to help others discover this time-saving book.

Plus, I appreciate helpful feedback and am always looking to provide more value to readers. Look forward to seeing your review!

This link will take you to the book's review page on Amazon: **www.JTMcKay.com/review5**

Thank YOU!

Made in United States
Troutdale, OR
08/12/2023